Running for Beginners

The Training Guide to Run Properly, Get in Shape and Enjoy Your Body

Peter Coleman

Table of Contents

Dear reader,

Thank you for choosing this book; I hope you can enjoy the reading.

Please, remember to write a review; I'm looking forward to know your opinion.

Peter Coleman

Introduction

Running has always been up there as far as exercise goes, and with new technology, it's easy to maintain a healthy physique once you get started. However, it is increasingly difficult to find time to run. A lot of careers now are often home or office-based, and these stationary settings do not give the body enough attention throughout the day, often leading to neglect. The term "couch potato" may have started as a gag, but more and more are falling into the sedentary trap.

Running is hard, at least to the general public. Many do not take the time to learn how to run because it takes more effort to get out on the road than stay home and kid yourself that you will break out the weights. Many also believe that running is boring, and other workouts are more beneficial. Because of this, running is often put aside for other forms of exercise or none at all. Running, though, is in our blood.

The human race has been running since the dawn of time. Hunters ran after prey to capture them and eat or skin. Even when farming became the thing to do, people remained in excellent shape working outside in the blazing sun for hours on end. As time went on, running was an important factor in winning or losing a battle, and stamina was considered a highly profitable attribute.

With the rise of the Olympics and other competitive sporting events, running became a staple, with strong men competing in both speed and distance tournaments. A young Greek soldier left the town of Marathon to travel to the city of Athens to deliver the news of the victory of the Battle of Marathon. The legend goes that, as soon as he made it to Athens and delivered the message, he fell dead. I can tell you with certainty that today's marathon runners would relate.

Time goes on and running has become less necessary for maintaining daily life but, we still compete for the running title at the Olympics every four years, and it has morphed into a great way to lose weight or maintain a level of fitness. Though we have come a long way from needing to run, the nature of running still exists within us.

Running is more important now than ever before. With the onslaught of fast-food restaurants on every corner and the stress of everyday life, it is essential to stay active and take care of your body. It is easy to make excuses, but there are even more reasons why you should head out the door and become a runner today.

This book was written to help people like you make running easier. *Running for Beginners: The Training Guide to Run Properly, Get in Shape and Enjoy Your Body* helps you understand what happens to your body when you run, how it can affect your life in positive ways, and how you can enjoy the time, even if the thought makes you sigh or "ugh". Running does not have to be hard; these chapters make it more natural to put your best foot forward and gain better health through running.

This book takes you through the reasons for running and why it is important for both your body and mind to begin. If you struggle from mental illness, exercise has been proven to help you create healthy hormones and chemicals in the brain, making your life easier and providing you with the brainpower you need to power through the day. Your body also receives the benefits of running by becoming leaner, helping both self-esteem and your overall mood. Everyone knows that running will help you live longer, but this book will guide you through the reasons why and how following these principles will make your body a better place in which to live.

Many people struggle with nutrition when they first begin the journey to health. Eating is one of the biggest parts of becoming fit, and it is often overlooked by new runners since many diets today differ in what is consumed and when. However, the nutrition in this book will guide you through proper ways to eat for running and the benefits you will receive when you follow the right regimen. Everything about eating is found in the *Running Commandments*, a list of ways I have provided in the text to improve your nutritional lifestyle.

Another important part of running is your equipment. Far from accessorizing the perfect outfit, runners need to know the ins and outs of shoes, how to pick the right pair, and how to know which pair is best for you. This book will walk you through becoming aware of what your body needs in all seasons and how to shop to improve your performance on the streets.

You will learn how to do warm-ups to effectively prepare your body for running. Warm-ups get your blood pumping and flowing through every part of your body and provide you with the punch you need to work out. You will receive instructions for common warm-ups and how they work different parts of your body. Cooldowns, after the completion of every workout are also important to make sure your muscles remain pliable and help prevent soreness over time. Following the guides to effective cooldowns in this book will help you stay injury-free.

Your running technique is what helps you prevent injury and will make running far more enjoyable. Considering these techniques as you run will make you a better runner and will improve timing, pace, and distance without negatively affecting the body. High-impact sports like running put a toll on the body if you are not doing it correctly. Using the whole body to run is just the beginning of understanding how to run well.

When injuries happen, and they will, it is helpful to know what they are and how to treat them quickly. *Running for Beginners: The Training Guide to Run Properly, Get in Shape and Enjoy Your Body* guides you through the most common injuries, what they are, and how to prevent them. Every new runner needs to understand the most common injuries to prevent imbalanced running and keep you on the go for years to come. Before you run, you will see the warning signs that will keep you from common traps.

Finally, this book contains eight programs that guide you through running whether you are just starting or have been at it for years. Each program provides solid advice to guide you through each week, how to focus your efforts and what to watch for while you run. These eight programs are the springboards for future running, and they provide solid techniques that will help you understand how to get the most out of your program.

Running is a highly social sport that encourages people from all walks of life to engage each other in new found techniques and commiserate in failures. Everyone in the running community is in place to help, lifting and supporting newcomers and cheering on those who have been running for years. When you join the running community, you will feel like part of a team from the physical and virtual interactions with those of all walks of life.

Countless books and blogs have been written to help beginners start their running careers on the right foot (pun intended). Thousands have added their voices to the crowd of those already in place who love to run and talk about it. Running competitions like races and marathons, bring people together to celebrate causes and to unite in their love of the sport. Olympians thrived on running, the simplest of sports, to compete for countries and to bring the world together in friendly competition.

Here you will be able to identify the techniques you need to become an excellent runner. You will also be able to identify how you can change yourself to have more fun on the track. Pounding the pavement should be neither difficult nor demanding of the body if you do it correctly. It all comes down to how to become the best you can be and go that extra mile (sorry) to make it a reality. The only one who can help you succeed is you, and the road is only impossible if you believe it to be. There is no reason why anyone should not run when they learn how and now is your chance to become the best version of yourself.

When you run, you run with the rest of the world, thanks to the internet. You can become a part of a world-wide event by using the techniques in this book to become a great runner. When you add the support of friends and family, it becomes easier to achieve your goals and become the runner you envision while reading these sentences. The best runners take one step at a time and learn to adjust to changes as they come. Rome was not built in a day, and neither will your desire to run. So, what are you waiting for? Lace-up your shoes, get out there and become the runner you know you can be.

Chapter 1: Why Run?

You have no doubt heard people say running is one of the best exercises to lose weight, get fit, and maintain a healthy physique. However, running can feel like the worst thing you can do to your body when you are panting like a dog and hacking up a lung. So, why in the world would you want to start running, an exercise that sometimes seems like it is more trouble than it is worth?

The hardest part about running is getting started. If you are new to running and feel like you do not know where to start, it can feel overwhelming, especially if you do not have a friend who has already been doing it for a long time. However, you may be surprised to know that, after the first few attempts, running gets much more comfortable and can make you feel like a million bucks.

These general reasons for running are enough to get most people out of the door. But that may not be the case for you, and that is okay, we are just getting started. There are many other reasons to go over that I guarantee will have you running for your shoes. You just need that first reason to get outside. Once you find your motivation to start life as a regular runner, it becomes that much easier to start your journey.

Mental Benefits

Unless you are well versed in running, you may not have known that running is highly beneficial to your mental health. When you feel like dying or can't catch a breath during a run, it may be hard to believe that your mind is actually getting healthier with each exercise, but it is true. In fact, the mental benefits are the main reasons that people stick with running for life.

So, what exactly does running do for your mind? Studies have shown that running can affect both mental illnesses and general exhaustion. Running allows people to overcome difficult obstacles in life by forcing them to act outside of a locked mindset. With the power of overcoming adversity, the body becomes more readily available for difficult challenges, making your life just that much more pleasant.

Running Decreases Depression

Depression is one of the most difficult mental illnesses to overcome, and it is one of the main reasons that runners set out. Depression can feel like a cage in which escape is impossible. After all, if you have depression, it feels as though the world is against you and the only place to feel safe is under the covers. Mental illness makes it difficult to find any motivation, so running may seem like the last place to find refuge during an episode.

However, if you do find the energy to make it out of bed, there are exceptional benefits to putting on those running shoes and heading outside. Runners get what is known as a two-fold benefit package. Not only do they receive the benefits of exercise, but they also receive advantages from being in nature. Unlike many other exercises, running can take you anywhere, making it a great way to keep you connected with nature.

Fresh air and sunlight are key to becoming a happy, healthier person. Because depression entices its sufferers to stay in the shadows, the energy of a closed environment inevitably plays a role in that trapped feeling. A change in environment has been proven to lift the moral and overall happiness of those who suffer from mental health issues. Vitamin D is one of the most common benefits of spending time in the sun, so putting on a pair of running shoes will allow you to get that necessary vitamin for free.

Many non-runners also feel a sense of entrapment in this activity. They feel as though pounding the pavement is lonely, and hardly the place to refresh your body if there is no emotional or physical contact with others. However, the running community is vast and always open to new people. Running does not have to be lonely. In fact, many use running as an excuse to get out and meet new people. Running is often a way of life for people, so most are happy to involve anyone who wants to join.

Those who suffer from depression often also feel a pull of emotions, causing their bodies to have a jittery sensation. Racing pulses and energy in muscles are common effects of depression. Running helps to alleviate those feelings by removing the bad energy from the body. When running, your body has a chance to move the energy in a healthy way. The body becomes able to release tension, and any emotions that drag you down or loosens your tight grip on reality.

Runners also often receive an additional incentive to perform in the form of a runner's high. Often seen as a myth, the runner's high does not get the recognition it deserves when discussing possible aids to depression. It is, however, far from a myth. In fact, it is born out of millennia of evolution for one purpose: to help the body overcome the aches and pains that come from excessive exercise.

There are three possible reasons for the runner's high. The first includes the theory that helpful chemicals are released, such as dopamine, serotonin, and norepinephrine. These chemicals release happy feelings in the body, making running that much easier. The second theory deals with the body's natural temperatures, and its change affects our moods positively. The third explanation for the runner's high is the release of a chemical called endocannabinoid. Yep, you read that right. Some believe that the runner's high deals out a compound that is associated with marijuana. So, when you head out on the race track, you are giving your body a healthy alternative to drugs, literally.

Alleviates Anxiety

Anxiety is one of the most common forms of mental illnesses in the United States. A study concluded that nearly one in every five people has been diagnosed with an anxiety disorder. And that statistic only applies to people who are diagnosed with a mental illness, as one-third of those actually come forward.

Anxiety causes a loss of focus and leaves the body in a constant fight-or-flight mode that prevents the brain from operating properly. In a fight-or-flight mode, all the blood that would have been reserved for brain function is now used in other parts of the body, which you can often feel in the form of heart palpitations. As a result, the brain is often left with little blood flow, causing light-headedness, panic, insomnia, and obsessions, just to name a few.

But what does this have to do with running? Like depression, anxiety causes hormones in the brain to either overproduce or underproduce certain chemicals that cause healthy brain functions. However, running causes the body to produce these chemicals while pounding the pavement. Endorphins, or the "feel-good" chemicals in your body, are produced due to high rates of metabolic activity. So, the harder you work, the more likely you are to receive these endorphins.

Another study suggests that improving the length of telomeres plays a significant role in the alleviation of stress. Telomeres are small particles in the body that prevent the fraying of chromosomes at their ends. Essentially, they act as plastic caps over the ends of the chromosomes. The length of these telomeres determines the health of the body. Consider the aglets at the ends of your shoelaces. Though they might not seem like the most important parts of the shoelace, they actually provide a sturdy, protective barrier that keeps your laces intact. Now consider their lengths. Extremely short aglets are hardly useful with woven shoelaces, and they often break off, causing the shoelaces to fray. Long aglets, on the other hand, prevent the laces from fraying and allow you to use those laces for many shoes to come.

Telomeres at the ends of chromosomes follow the same principle. Telomeres typically shorten over the years, which implies they are related to aging. Shortened telomeres lead to health problems such as stress. However, even a short time of vigorous exercise can help lengthen the telomeres, effectively acting as a healing agent. According to Elizabeth Fernandez, "vigorous physical activity as brief as 42 minutes over three days, similar to federally recommended levels, can protect individuals from the effects of stress by reducing its impact on telomere length" (2010). The more activity, the greater the chance for mental health. Running, as one of those vigorous exercises, plays an integral role in the betterment of mental health.

Improves Learning

The brain receives more blood to the brain when the body stops focusing on a fight-or-flight mode and instead relieves the tensions built from anxiety and depression. It would only make sense, then, that the additional blood to the brain from running would affect the way you learn. You are better able to remember details, and the mind can return to its production of endorphins.

In an experiment conducted by Bernward Winter, running was used as a method by which to determine the effects of exercise on the brain. All subjects were tested both before to and after the completion of a vigorous running exercise. Before running, bilingual subjects were asked to translate a phrase, memory, and attention. They were then subjected to running on a treadmill with an increase of 1.2 mph after every minute. They ran until they were tired and retook the tests. The results showed a significant rise in cognitive speed (Winter et al., 2007). The bilingual subjects were able to translate at an accelerated rate, and they could better retain the words they learned after the exercise.

Other studies related to subjects' brain functions determined that running is one of the best ways to improve your health. So, not only is aerobic exercise highly effective in improving learning and memory, but running provides a cheap option that is highly accessible and yet highly profitable. Candace L. Hogan determined, "evidence for the benefits of exercise on both affective experience and cognitive performance points to exercise as an effective, low-cost intervention for improving both affective and cognitive health." The health of the brain is determined, therefore, by how the body is used.

Since it was proven that only a short amount of exercise yields impressive results regarding learning, just imagine how much continuous activity can do for the mind and body. When starting to run, it is unnecessary to run six miles on the first day. Instead, work up to longer bouts, and you will see the improvement in brain functions over time.

Prevents Brain Aging

You see it in everyday life. The brain tends to age dramatically over time, and many brain functions slow. Since the increase of telomeres from physical fitness keeps the body from aging rapidly, it only makes sense that the brain would see some resistance to aging as well.

A study recorded in Time Magazine in 2012 determines the validity of the suggestion that exercise stops or decreases the shrinkage of brains. Scottish scientists tested over 600 people aged 70, asking them their habits, including exercise and brain games. Then they took MRIs of all participants and noted the habits they had. Three years later, they brought new MRIs and recorded the exercise and brain games that each participant had mentioned. Those that were more active mind and body showed a lowered shrinkage rate.

What is surprising about the study, however, is its connection to exercise. Though both exercise and brain games decreased brain shrinkage, exercise was determined to be the greatest factor in retaining brain matter. Exercises as simple as walking proved to help the brain maintain its high level of functionality.

Those who exercised the most showed the most improvement in brain functions and the least shrinkage, which means that more intense aerobic exercise proved the most beneficial. Even as a running beginner, you can receive the benefits of a healthy mind through determination and commitment to the sport.

Helps Heal Brain from Substance Abuse

Substance abuse is one of the most difficult hurdles to overcome in any person's life. Many who start do not succeed in ridding themselves of the addiction the first or 20th time.

Cravings are some of the most intense feelings associated with substance abuse, and something as small as seeing condensation on the outside of a cold beer can cause relapse.

For those who struggle with substance abuse, it can be very difficult to overcome the constant need for a stimulus. And that is where running can help. The high experienced during running can act as an alternative to drug-simulated highs. Dopamine is one of the most effective natural chemicals in the brain that make the mind feel "happy," and the one most commonly produced by drugs. Running also produces dopamine and other chemicals, as a natural alternative.

Studies have shown that running has proven effective for countering the effects of drug usage. Dr. Wendy Lynch used this principle when working with rats addicted to cocaine. She and her team exposed the rats to a large supply of cocaine, effectively addicting each subject. Each cage was outfitted with a cocaine supply lever that, when pushed, would deliver the drug. After the addiction, she then cut their supply for two weeks. The control group was not allowed any form of stimulus or anything else that would help them release their frustrations. The test group was given a wheel in which they were allowed to run for two hours every day.

The rats that had access to a running wheel showed a remarkably large improvement compared to those who did not. They were documented as pressing the lever 35% less than the control group. When cocaine was introduced to the group again, those with the running wheel pressed the lever 45% less than those without the wheel (Daniloff, 2017). The results indicate that both groups of rats, exposed to the same amount of cocaine, had radically different results based on one test difference: running.

Another study conducted for marijuana addiction showed much the same results. Each subject, 12 in total, described themselves as addicts to marijuana and expressed no desire for rehabilitation. Over two weeks, Dr. Peter Martin required that each subject run on a treadmill for 10 to 30 minutes every day. By the end of the first week, he saw a considerable change in their addiction levels, noting that their cravings dropped by 50% (Boerner, 2011). Though the experiment was conducted over two weeks, Dr. Martin declared there was no need for further work after one week. The results of running had proven themselves.

Running is far from the only way to deal with drug addiction, but it has proven to be one of the most effective. The brain is essentially rewired with every run to become more able to deal with the effects of difficult drug addiction. When running, the body becomes less dependent on outside sources and instead focuses on natural chemicals the brain produces.

Many addicts use running as an outlet for cravings and other addictive behaviors. In fact, some rehabilitation centers actually use running as a method to overcome drug addiction. Some facilities in the United States, Canada, and Ireland require "rock-bottom" addicts to train for running competitions as part of their treatment. People who start their recoveries with running also often see the benefits throughout life. They continue to run, although many of their regular cravings for their drugs of choice have largely subsided.

Improves Creativity

Just as running can improve brain function, it is also essential in connecting the dots creatively. Some of the most famous writers, painters, and artists find that walking or running significantly improves their ability to think. The brain reacts favorably to running and often creates new connections in the brain, leading to understanding and creative intelligence.

Through research, scientists have established that the creation of new cells is related to exercise. Exercise also improves the lifetimes of those brain cells. As discussed previously, the brain experiences an improvement in brain function and health when exposed to exercise, and memory improves with higher levels of aerobic activity. The hippocampus shows an increase in size with regular exercise.

That is a lot of information, but it all comes down to one simple explanation: the brain is significantly improved with aerobic exercise. The hippocampus is where creativity dwells, so the larger your hippocampus, the more likely you are to think both logically and creatively. After all, who would not want a bigger brain?

Because running also aids in helping those with anxiety and depression, it has become a key factor in creativity. Anxiety and depression bog down the mind with debilitating thoughts, but those that run often feel those negative feelings fade as healthy chemicals are introduced to the brain. The mind can then become clear, allowing the mind to focus on creative activities.

Consistency is also key to a happier brain. Though taking any time out of your day to run is a marketable achievement, developing a schedule for your workouts can improve your creativity over time. Author Haruki Murakami uses a routine to help him write some of his best work. If you have read one of his novels, then you know that they are intricate and long. Each day, he spends several hours writing, then runs at least 6 miles or swims (Presland, 2017). He attributes much of his success to running because it helps him open his mind.

Those who struggle with creativity may see a potential increase in brain activity after a workout. With this in mind, it hardly seems logical to forgo a day from the gym. Even if you believe that you are primarily left-brained, studies have shown that exercise gives rise to images of the future, allowing the mind to think more effectively.

Running also helps the brain become more focused. Running acts as a cleansing ritual, providing a clean slate after exercise. The willpower necessary to complete long marathons easily translates into everyday life. When you develop a solid nutritional regime and add exercise to the mix, the body becomes regulated to work with the energy it is given.

Boosts Self-Esteem

It is no secret that running builds self-esteem. As the body starts to acclimatize to running, it builds stronger and leaner muscles. Consistent running will undoubtedly change the way that the body appears and functions, ultimately leading to more body satisfaction. Seeing yourself become a more fit version of yourself is the first step in gaining self-esteem.

However, the changing body is not the only reason for a boost in self-esteem. In a study done by Dr. Dorothy L. Schmalz, 197 girls ages 9 through 13 showed a greater increase in self-confidence when they competed at higher capacities than their counterparts. Over ten years, they studied children who answered the question, "Would you rather stay inside and watch tv or play, or would you rather spend time outdoors to play" (Schmalz, 2007). Those that responded with wanting to spend more time outdoors at the ages of 11 or 13 showed an increased level of self-esteem of those who preferred to spend more time inside.

The study concludes that those who spend more time outdoors generally have a greater self-esteem boost as they get older because they are more active. They are receiving natural endorphins that aid in the reduction of anxiety and depression, preventing early cases of self-esteem issues. The study also showed a lack of dependence on the BMI, which means that the children who were larger and enjoyed spending time outdoors more than indoors showed the same amount of body positivity.

Any aerobic exercise is indeed good for both the body and mind, but running is particularly helpful. Running outdoors ensures that the body receives both fresh air and sunlight, two factors that also improve mood. The sense of accomplishment after running also adds to positive attitudes. Those who do not participate in activities are often less likely to feel confident due to a sense of frustration from lack of effort.

Physical Benefits

No list of benefits for running would be complete without mentioning the physical benefits that come from running. After all, that is why many people choose to run in the first place.

Running has had a significant history, which is mostly due to its accessibility. Sports such as the discus, boxing, and gymnastics have been around for millennia; they do not hold a candle to running's past. Humans are not the fastest runners in the animal kingdom, but we are one of the best species at endurance running. Few animals can sustain a steady pace for a marathon's distance, all thanks to evolution.

Our early ancestors were not born to run, but they developed the ability over time for survival. The human body contains muscles in the legs that allow us to store energy and then release it in a spring-like explosion that is unique to just about any other creature except the cheetah (Stipp, 2012). Our bodies also house some of the best heat-releasing mechanisms, allowing us to expel heat through sweating, a unique trait in humans. Because of evolution, our bodies can handle long-distance running. We are meant to run.

It may be possible to run long distances, but why should you do it? Well, besides pushing you to your limits, running influences the body in a good way. Running affects your body by aiding in heart health, achieving a leaner figure, and adding days, weeks, or even years to your lifespan. It is also one of the most applauded types of exercises because of its ability to influence the whole body at the same time. Because it is built into our DNA, running provides the body with extraordinary strength and improves the body over time.

Strengthens Bones and Muscles

Many people believe that running negatively affects the body. The pain experienced by first-time and even long-time runners makes it hard to disagree with that statement, especially when you are out on the pavement feeling every step. The impact on joints and bones from constant stress while running is the supporting argument for running causing osteoporosis, a disease that causes the density of the bones to decrease. Running is often linked to this disease because those who suffer knee and hip injuries are more likely to get this disease.

However, running itself is responsible for the strengthening of joints and cartilage. In a study done by Paul T. Williams (2013), he used feedback from nearly 90,000 runners to determine if osteoporosis was caused by running. Over 50,000 of these participants ran in marathons annually, and each were divided into groups to determine if the number of races the runners competed in aided in the development of osteoporosis. The results, conducted on runners who ran in one to five marathons annually, showed no direct correlation to the disease. Of course some people ran more often than others, but they were at no greater risk of developing osteoporosis than those who ran less.

Another high cause of osteoporosis is weight. So, instead of showing a direct correlation to osteoporosis, running is a preventative measure. Runners lose weight due to long bouts of exercise, reducing risk. Runners who are not careful to prevent injuries often experience them, so it is extraordinarily important to follow proper stretching techniques.

Running is often known as an open-chain exercise. This means that the body experiences stress contact with the ground. When your feet hit the pavement, they are making direct contact with a hard surface, putting stress on the bones. This jarring in the body allows for blood to flow easier through the body during exercise. Calcium in the bloodstream is then absorbed into the bones, strengthening them.

Runners may also experience better joint health. Because you build muscle as you run, joints are cushioned from each impact, generally showing better health than those who do not exercise. Many people associate arthritis with running because it is a high-impact sport, but studies have shown that there is no correlation between running and arthritis. Runners are often cautioned to include strength training with their regular workouts to build joint strength. The key to maintaining good joint health is to take care of your body. Though there is always some excuse for not grabbing your running shoes, injury is one of the leading causes of arthritis. Just as running can be incredibly helpful for building joint strength, it can also cause a lot of damage if not treated properly.

Decreases Unhealthy Food Cravings

Just as running is extremely helpful in overcoming substance abuse, so it is with unhealthy food cravings. Unhealthy food, though not often seen as an addiction, affects some people more than others in ways similar to drug addiction. Sugars, fats, and salts can become highly addictive over time, and it is often difficult to stop once consuming these foods becomes a way of life.

Running can curb unhealthy food addiction. Those who ran showed a greater inclination to choose healthy foods after running than those who chose not to exercise. A study conducted determined how the brain was affected after running. Using males who ran at high speeds for an hour, scientists took brain scans while the men looked at images of food. Those who had run at an accelerated rate for an hour displayed fewer cravings than those who did not. Essentially, the mind becomes less interested in unhealthy foods after high-intensity exercise. Hunger was suppressed, and the hormones usually created when hungry displayed lower levels.

If you are new to running, you have likely not experienced the pain of maintaining an unhealthy diet when exercising consistently. It is common to feel stomach aches when eating too many unhealthy foods throughout a running program. This alone is a significant reason for many to abandon processed sugars, fats, and salts and base their diet on the consumption of high protein and greens. Not only does the body have more energy when consuming healthier foods, but it feels better overall.

Allows for Better Sleep

For those who have exercised consistently in the past, it should come as no surprise that aerobic exercise helps you sleep better. After all, your body starts to wear out after long periods of activity.

We use our bodies far less than we have in the past. The first humans were hunters and gatherers that had to use both strength and endurance to survive in both harsh and lush environments. The body had to hold up as those who gathered food frequently bent, twisted, and moved throughout the day. Hunters needed stamina and athletic ability to receive prey. Even as humans evolved, the body continued to work in different functions: farming, building, sailing, just to name a few. It was not uncommon to move all day every day. However, the last few centuries have shown a shift in basic bodily function. With machines, we can stay in one place, and the use of our minds has become an important skill in survival. The human race just does not get the exercise it used to. Exercising, therefore, is an essential part of daily life, and sleep is better when it is added to a daily routine. Running, one of the most basic of human exercises is a great place to start.

A study conducted at Northwestern University used a group of adults with insomnia and no record of exercise to determine how sleeping problems would improve after consistent exercise. The group was divided in two, the control group that would not exercise and the group that would. The study concluded after 16 weeks, and those who had exercised saw marked improvements in their sleeping patterns and quality of sleep.

According to psychological studies, however, sleep is not immediately improved after running once. It can take weeks or months for the benefits of better sleep to kick in. Many who start their exercise journeys believe that they will reap the benefits of sleep aid after a single week. Though it might help you moderately, you will not see significant results until you begin to exercise more consistently. Though that may be unhappy news for some, the study did show that there was a correlation over time. The key to good sleep, therefore, is sticking with an exercise routine.

Since running is also highly effective for those with anxiety and depression, you may see a change in your sleeping patterns after just a few sessions. Both mental illnesses prevent the mind from shutting down, which starts the sleeping process. The chemicals released after running allows the body to experience an upswing in mood, which will help the mind overcome difficult obstacles.

Helps You Live Longer

Perhaps one of the most common benefits of running is the fact that it aids in healing a body and allowing you to live longer. Many believe that hitting the track often and for long periods aids in a long life, but even a little can give you some extra years.

Australian researchers studied fourteen studies conducted about the effects of running on almost a quarter of a million participants. The studies ranged from short time frames (5.5 years) to longer (35 years). Each study marked what happened to participants after they ran consistently or inconsistently for the years of the study. Perhaps unsurprisingly, the research showed that those who ran more showed a healthier life than those who ran less. In all, the data "The collective data showed that any amount of running was associated with a 30% lower risk of death from heart disease, and a 23% lower risk of death from cancer" (Preidt, 2019). In essence, those who practiced a healthier lifestyle through running had healthier bodies.

Of course, that doesn't seem like news, but the research determined health in a different capacity as well. Most research showed that it does not matter how much time you spend running to gain health benefits as long as you make it a part of your week. The study showed that running, one of the most accessible forms of exercise, only one hour every week was enough to make them healthier.

This should not discourage you from running longer, if you can. The studies also showed that there was an increase in health benefits to those who chose to run more. Essentially, if you want to increase your overall health and the possibility of living longer, put in the time to run more. Running lowers the risk of high blood pressure, obesity, type 2 diabetes, and high cholesterol. The more prone you are to have these issues, the more important it is to run consistently.

Since running in many vocations is swiftly coming to an end, it is imperative that running becomes a part of our culture now. Obesity is a common problem, and sitting all day and eating unhealthy foods are becoming a daily part of life. To become a healthier nation, many scientists suggest that running is the answer. It is easy, accessible, and essential to the overall health of the world.

Chapter 2: Nutrition

Think of when you were a kid, and running seemed easy as you were always running after something outside. As you got older, you probably experienced aches and pains that kept you from spending as much time outdoors. Though getting a stitch in your knee didn't keep you from playing outside, as you got older, taking it easy became more common when anything physical went wrong. If this sounds familiar, you are not alone. Many new runners often fail because it can seem overwhelming to juggle a proper diet with the right amount of exercise.

Any runner will tell you that one of the most important parts of running is the food you eat. This influences the way you perform, and eating too much or too little of anything can be detrimental to your health and performance. Stomach aches and other pains are common when not satisfying nutritional health. Just as limbs require warming up before strenuous exercise, the body's organs require proper sustenance to make them more efficient.

Eating for running, though, is slightly different than eating for health. The food you consume when running gives you energy you need and the nutritional benefits for endurance and high-intensity running.

The Running Commandments

Even if you have always kept a good diet, you may still feel your body start to drag when you run. The extra exercise and impact that running has on your body is one of the reasons why you feel this way. Many runners choose to take supplements with meals to compensate for mineral loss while running. So, to get the most out of what you eat, follow what I call the Running Commandments.

Eat More

It should not be counterintuitive that you need to eat more when you start exercising more. You start to burn more calories, and you need to replace what you have lost. If you are running to lose weight, you still need to eat more than if you are following a basic diet. Give your body the fuels it needs without overcompensating for caloric loss.

Carbohydrates

If you hope to run in a marathon, it is essential to find the right foods and eat in larger quantities than before you started running. Before you start a long run, load up on carbohydrates at least 12 hours before you start to run. Cramping often happens when trying to push that time limit, so stick to a reasonable time limit. Carbohydrates are the easy to access fuels in the food kingdom. They act as small energy pockets that are temporary activators. Eating too many carbs and not burning them off after a one to two day time frame, though, converts those carbs to fat.

Runners should add 100 calories to their diet for every mile they run. If you are unsure of how much you can run, test your limits and take note. The majority of those calories should be carbs. Plan for the number of miles you will run and determine how many more miles you can add to your exercise routine. Good carbs for running include:

- Potatoes
- Apples
- Bagels
- Carrots
- Wheat bread
- Bananas
- Cereal
- Pasta
- Macaroni
- Yams

You can consume larger quantities of most of these carbs, and it is a good idea to do so. For example, instead of eating two slices of white bread, two apples hold roughly the same number of calories, and they are healthier. Instead of eating an 8 oz bag of chips, you could theoretically eat six cups of pasta.

Protein

Protein has become a hot button topic for several years, and there is no secret that loading up on proteins will help keep your bones healthy. Protein shakes are popular, and it has become common practice to eat meats and proteinated vegetables before a race.

It is wise to eat proteins as part of your running routine, but only in moderate amounts. Proteins are responsible for tissue repair, so high-impact sports, such as running, require proteins to help repair your muscles. But there is only so much protein you can consume before it stops being beneficial. Deborah Shulman, a nutritionist with a doctorate in physiology, states that the best way to get the most out of your protein consumption is to follow the 30/30 rule: Consume less than 30 grams of protein in less than 30 minutes after a workout (Bruning, 2017). You should be aiming for around 20 grams of protein after a workout, but this rule makes it a little easier to remember.

Finding the right kind of protein is essential in creating a balanced diet. Of course, when many think of proteins, they think of red meat, but that is not always the best option. They usually come with a large portion of fat, which can be damaging to your diet. Instead, look for proteins like:

- Legumes (peanuts, etc.)
- Farm-raised, lean, chicken
- Tofu
- Yogurt
- Beans
- Peas
- Fish
- Eggs
- Cheese
- Nuts

Eating enough protein should not feel like a burden. Experiment with different proteins to find out which you enjoy the most. This will make it easier for you to keep up with and provide you with more energy throughout the day. I can't stress this enough: Do not go overboard with protein consumption. Like carbohydrates, proteins will turn to fat if they are not used.

The general rule for the right amount of protein consumption per day is based on weight. For every pound you weigh, you should be eating about one gram per pound if you want to gain muscle. The amount of protein you need is also determined by the type of running you are doing. Short distance runners need fewer grams of protein than long distance runners.

Fats
Many diets today believe that you should either consume next to no fats or you should consume massive quantities.

However, to maintain a healthy body, you must find a middle ground. Fats should make up approximately 20-30% of your daily intake. The key to consuming fats is to find the right kinds of fats. Look for unsaturated fats such as these:

- Salmon
- Avocado
- Vegetable oil
- Nuts
- Whole eggs
- Natural peanut butter
- Chia seeds
- Pumpkin
- Sunflower
- Tuna
- Flaxseed

Since many diet fads insist that fats are bad and should be avoided, it can be hard to remember to eat them. However, you may see a significant change in the way you feel when you run if you consume them regularly. Fats make running easier, and they improve stamina. So, especially if you are a first time runner, take the time to figure out the best types of fats for you to eat.

Processed sugar is an enemy to many, mostly because it acts almost as a drug, making you come back to it again and again. However, if you eat the right fats in the right quantities, you will see a significant decrease in sugar cravings. Avoid any products that claim to be fat-free because they usually contain more processed sugars, which will pull you back into the vicious cycle.

Foods with fat are healthier than their low-fat alternatives...in small portions. Foods with full fats have more nutrition than those without. Without full fats, you are missing out on vital vitamins and minerals such as B-12, omega-3 fatty acids, and many others. So, if you question whether or not you should eat that egg yolk, the answer is yes.

Fats also aid in injury prevention. While fats are not the miracle cure to remaining injury-free, a study at the University of Buffalo determined that those who suffered the most from injuries consistently consumed fewer calories from fat than their counterparts. Many female students in the study believed that fats were damaging to their bodies, so they consumed them in smaller amounts. The study determined, however, the opposite.

Plan Your Diet

If you have started a diet that never took off, you are not alone. Many a diet have failed due to a lack of planning. The problem is that many people do not know how to make a meal plan. However, thanks to the internet, it is becoming easier to break down foods and recipes to find the best nutrition plan for you. Meal planning is personal, especially if you are doing it for a person with allergies, but there are three main steps to follow to create your perfect meal plan: create or find recipes, create a shopping list, and prep.

Create or Find Recipes
If you are crafty or love to cook, this is a great place to start. Though there are thousands of cookbooks available, some of the best recipes are free on the internet. All you have to do is narrow down your search to find the best options. Of course, that is often easier said than done, but there is always a way to satisfy both your nutritional needs and your budget.

First, find ingredients that will satisfy you. What sort of starches, fruits, vegetables, proteins, and fats meet your nutritional needs? If you have a favorite vegetable, find a recipe that either includes or is centered around that vegetable. Look for proteins that you enjoy and offer nutritional benefits.

Next, determine how much time you have to make these recipes, it may seem like fun to create a five-course meal or tasty to marinate something for eight hours, remember it also has to fit in your schedule somewhere. Also, keep track of your eating habits. If you are constantly heading out for fast food because you have no time to cook your own meals, find recipes that either do not take long to prepare or require little effort, like slow-cooker meals.

Find enough recipes that will last you for at least a week. If you plan to use ingredients that spoil easily, find ways to eat them sooner. Invest in quality Tupperware to keep all of your ingredients fresh, and freeze those that can be frozen.

Create a Shopping List

Unless you are a super-shopper, chances are that you do not enjoy heading to the grocery store. This is one of the best reasons why you should plan meals for the week ahead of time. And there is a process to set up the best grocery list.

First, create a master list. This includes all the ingredients you need for your recipes. The list should even include everything you think you have in your kitchen, but more on that in a bit. Next, go through the entire list and cross off everything you already have in your kitchen. Remember, though, that your list may include ingredients that need to be filled, so make sure to check on your supplies.

Next, create your grocery list. After you are done crossing everything off, either rewrite what you need to get or just keep the list as is. Next, group everything by where you will find it in the grocery store. You are less likely to buy on impulse if you have a list of everything you need that is conveniently located to take away from wandering. If you are more interested in digital lists, there are some apps that will group them for you, saving you time.

Prep

Pick the best day to do your prep. Because Friday is the beginning of the weekend, it is common to use it as your prep day. Have some fun with it and try to find the best ways to add flavor to your food. For food that can hold up in the freezer, designate containers just for this. Many slow-cooker meals are freezable, so you may find it easier to plan a month of meals and freeze the ingredients.

Eat More Often

If you spend a lot of time on the couch, you know the feeling of always wanting to eat. You can use this to your advantage. Instead of eating three large meals every day, consider eating five small meals, and make time for healthy snacks. You will be able to keep up the energy you need throughout the day without overdoing it at mealtime.

Cravings are the curse of runners. They are often associated with unhealthy foods and having a diet that restricts you to three meals often resulting in relapse as once you start to eat, your hunger grows. Separating meals prevents cravings from setting in if you are using the right formula.

First, separate your meals into groups based on their nutritional value. For example, put vegetables in one group, proteins in another, and fruits in another. Your meals need to last you through the day, so organize them according to the most energy you will receive from eating them. Fruits have natural sugars that provide energy, so eat fruits for the first or second meal. Many suffer from a lack of energy due to protein deficiency, so it may be wise to consider proteins for your first or second meals as well. Vegetables produce vitamins that are important to the body, so add these to any meal throughout the day.

Second, create plans for your meals based on your activities. If you run in the morning, eat protein shortly after. If you have a moderate office job, you may want to save your protein for the evening. Experiment with which foods give you the most energy throughout the day. Journal your results to find the best meals and to count your calories.

Take Supplements

Even if you have devoted your life to keeping a nutritious diet, it is tough to get all the vitamins and minerals that you need. That is partially why the vitamin business is steadily booming. Taking the right supplements will help you not only perform better when running, but you will also see a change in your life in other ways. Taking the suggested vitamins will make you feel more awake, energized, and focused.

But how do you know which supplements are the right ones? With so many websites online full of self-proclaimed experts, it can be difficult to decipher what will actually help you achieve the results you seek. Before starting any regimen, contact a doctor. If you take too much of any supplement, you may start to feel worse, which is the opposite of the running nutrition goal. Stop what you are doing if you receive negative results. When running, however, it is best to know the right kinds of supplements to get your desired results.

BCAAs

Branch-chain amino acids (BCAAs), are amino acids found in food or in external supplements that help the body produce proteins. Bodybuilders use them because they allow the body to gain muscle quickly. However, recently they have also shown promise for long-distance runners. Long-distance runners often need more protein than those who only run for short distances because they lack the energy to endure. Marathon runners commonly use BCAAs to keep up their strengths during the racing season.

BCAAs are also commonly used to combat fatigue and other illnesses. They also aid in muscle recovery. Muscles tear during high-intensity weight training and long-distance running, and BCAAs aid in relieving the soreness after hard work. It also helps with weight loss and gaining lean muscle. Another benefit of BCAAs is its ability to produce energy from proteins previously consumed. BCAAs speed up the process to keep you running for longer. So, if you are feeling sluggish, it may be time to grab the supplement from the local drug store or eat some of the following foods:

- Red meat
- Soybeans
- Corn
- Fish
- Eggs
- Lentils
- Nuts
- Chicken
- Brown rice
- Dairy

Whey Protein

You can easily find whey protein in a drug store, as protein shakes are some of the most popular forms of this supplement, and it is common to see them in an array of flavors. Best of all, it helps you reach your protein goal without resorting to preparing a meal every time.

Just like BCAAs, whey protein is useful in the construction of muscles. Running takes a toll on muscles. Whey protein promotes healthy healing of those muscles while giving you the strength to continue training. If you plan to run long distances, use the 30/30 rule to determine how much whey protein to consume. Remember overeating protein will cause remaining molecules to convert to fat.

Whey protein also shows promising results regarding high blood pressure and type 2 diabetes. While there is not a significant change when applied to patients with these problems, whey protein makes a difference. Whey protein aids in moderating blood pressure, so it is effective in creating small amounts of insulin for the body. It has also shown positive results when tested with inflammatory bowel disease in rats. Though all of these benefits of whey protein show extraordinary results, you should not use it exclusively as a source of treatment.

Multivitamins

Multivitamins are not the miracle all-in-one pills that they are believed to be, but they are helpful in a pinch. Multivitamins hold the daily dosage amount for each vitamin listed in the pill, but taking too much of a single supplement can be dangerous. If you are eating properly, you should already have all of those vitamins in your diet. Read the amounts on the label before starting on any new multivitamin.

If you spend a lot of time out on the track, especially long-distance runners, multivitamins can be a good supplement to make part of your regimen. Long-distance runners do not always take all vitamins they require for a long running bout, so it may be helpful.

Glutamine

Glutamine is less popular than other supplements because it is an amino acid that occurs naturally in the bloodstream. However, many people do not have sufficient levels of glutamine in their systems. This shortage can cause feelings of fatigue and excessive soreness; this is what you need for long-distance running. Glutamine is often heavily depleted after an intense workout session, so adding the supplement to your diet can help with recovery.

Glutamine is also responsible for helping 'leaky gut', ulcers, and gastronomical issues. Leaky gut syndrome often causes allergies, irritable bowel syndrome, low energy, joint pain, thyroid issues, and muscle fatigue, which all play significant roles in the body's health. Taking additional supplements help the body recover naturally. Glutamine also aids in gastronomical health and rebuilding from poor health.

Along with others on this list, glutamine aids in the construction of muscles. Glutamine is an amino acid that builds protein, providing the body with the building blocks for muscle recovery. In addition, glutamine aids in weight loss. The after-burn effect, which is the burning of calories after a workout is completed, is largely due to glutamine. It provides a fat-burning reaction in conjunction with muscle building.

Doctors suggest that you use glutamine supplements sparingly and consult with a specialist first. Though it is highly beneficial to long-distance running, many foods provide you with the glutamine supply you need without resorting to a pill. Also, relying too much on supplements may cause your natural supply to dwindle and unable to regenerate naturally. Instead, try these foods to build up supply:

- Meat
- Milk
- Seafood
- Nuts
- Cabbage
- Eggs
- Beans
- Protein drinks

L-Carnitine

L-carnitine is a supplement already found in the body right down to the cellular level, and it is essential for healthy living. Mitochondria, the powerhouse of the cell, assists in energy production, and carnitine transports fatty acids to the mitochondria, allowing it to convert the acids into energy. Theoretically, the more L-carnitine you have in your body, the faster your body can produce energy. Carnitine also aids in muscle recovery, which means that it will help you overcome soreness. All in all, carnitine, which comes from meats and proteins, is essential in quick energy production.

If you have followed bodybuilding in the past, you may recognize the supplement carnitine. Muscle builders have been using it for quite some time to build muscle. But what happens when you take L-carnitine without bodybuilding? Unlike the other supplements on this list, carnitine is not recommended for weight loss. It helps you build muscle, not shed fat.

However, endurance runners use the supplement all the time. Carnitine helps athletes overcome difficult training periods, and it allows them to workout longer. Though there are some controversies concerning the effects of carnitine supplements, many studies agree that it improves performance. In a study done by the Journal of the International Society of Sports, a small group of women were tested for potential effects. Each group was given a pill: either a placebo or a carnitine supplement. After a few weeks, the women who took the supplement showed a substantial improvement over a three-mile run (Abundance & Health, 2018). This study took place in a limited time frame. Prolonged exposure to the supplement will yield better results.

Studies suggest that only 4 grams of carnitine are necessary to see results. Of course, like any other supplement, it takes time to sink into your system, but many saw an approximate improvement of 35%. The effectiveness also relies on the distance length for each run.

Fish Oil or Krill Oil

Fish and krill oil has been used for centuries for the simple reason that they offer many helpful benefits. Not everyone likes to eat fish, let alone every day. However, the Omega-3 fatty acids produced from fish are some of the most healthy you can receive in any supplement. Many choose to forego the fish meal altogether and simply purchase the product at a drugstore.

Krill are small shrimp-like creatures that are often associated with whales as a primary food source. They are extremely common in the ocean, which makes the appeal that much greater. The oil they produce allows humans to break down fatty acids into supplements that are easy to digest. Fish oil does the same thing, but some believe that it does not have the same potency. Before you choose one, test them out to find the right one for you as these products work differently with different people. For example, you may love fish oil, and a friend prefers krill oil.

Both oils are highly beneficial to running. Krill and fish oils are known for improving cardiovascular health, reducing the chances of heart attacks and strokes. They also lower bad cholesterol and increase good cholesterol, which reduces overall inflammation in blood vessels. Since your heart is frequently put to the test when running, it is important to maintain a healthy heart for running long distances.

You may also see changes in your overall mental health. Fish and krill oils are proven to improve depression and anxiety, and it is commonly used during menstruation for women to aid in relieving cramps. This is because it reduces inflammation in the body, making movement easier. These oils also help with joint pain, muscle recovery, and endurance. The body uses Omega-3 fatty acids to maintain healthy bodily functions, making running more comfortable.

If you are new to fish and krill oil, consult a doctor before starting any new regimen; those who have thin blood may notice adverse effects when taking this supplement. Start your supply at only 500 mg, and read the labels to determine the best quality of oils before beginning.

Calcium

Calcium is one of the most important supplements you could take. After all, they aid in bone growth and joint strength. But, does it make a significant difference in the way you can perform on the track? A study conducted by John Lappe showed that consuming more calcium helped to prevent stress fractures. Stress fractures are small cracks in the bone that occur during high-intensity sessions or frequent use. They also cause severe bruising in the bone, which can make them extremely painful.

Lappe used over 300 women in his study to determine if taking additional calcium and vitamin D supplements aided in preventing the stress fractures. Vitamin D was included because it helps in breaking down calcium. One group received a placebo, and the other received vitamin D and calcium supplements. Though the test group did receive stress fractures when performing high-intensity sports, they received approximately 20% less than the control group.

The study further suggests that the amount of time out running did not determine whether the subjects would receive stress fractures. Instead, it depended almost solely on the muscle and bone density of all participants. Therefore, those who received more calcium and vitamin D showed a more improved bone structure, confirming that adding this supplement is essential for those who do not receive enough.

Zinc and Magnesium

Zinc and magnesium are some of the most plentiful minerals in our bodies, and they are also some of the most essential. Zinc is responsible for bone health, a healthy immune system, and healthy aerobic exercise. Magnesium is responsible for your body's metabolism and ability to recover quickly. Both are highly available in other foods, but they are also commonly absent in the body if not taking supplements due to poor eating habits.

An absence of zinc is often highly evident due to the possible symptoms of hair loss, appetite loss, white marks on the nails, diarrhea, poor eyesight, or bad memory. Many athletes lose zinc through sweat, so maintaining a healthy supply of iron in the body is more difficult. However, these foods commonly hold zinc:

- Meat
- Legumes
- Shellfish
- Nuts
- Seeds
- Dairy
- Whole grains
- Eggs
- Dark chocolate

If, however, you do not have the right supplements in your diet, take external supplements to aid in your recovery. When doing so, you may notice an increase in athletic performance. Zinc makes the body better at producing energy for exercise, so adding it to your supplement list may be necessary.

Loss of magnesium is detrimental to bodily health, and it is no surprise why: It is included in most bodily functions. Unlike many other supplements, it cannot hurt to take more magnesium, as long as you are careful with the amounts. Magnesium aids in reducing inflammation, so without it, you may feel sluggish, preventing you from running your best.

Once you have finished your run, magnesium works on repairing muscle. Without more magnesium, you may experience spasms and feel weaker than normal. Though there are not many sources that have studied the athletic benefits of taking magnesium as a supplement, the few that have shown little correlation between taking more magnesium and performing better as an athlete. However, it aids your general health, so it does inadvertently help. Natural sources of magnesium include:

- Baked beans
- Fruits
- Nuts
- Seeds
- Dark chocolate
- Tofu
- Spinach
- Kale
- Seafood

A deficiency in magnesium is also often very apparent. It often leads to numbness, vomiting, spasms, loss of appetite, and nausea, so ask a doctor if you experience any of these problems.

Iron

Iron deficiencies are some of the most common in runners. Surprisingly, this has little at all to do with running but a great deal to do with diet. Iron may not make up a large portion of minerals, but it is essential in maintaining a healthy body. Many who have this deficiency feel tired often, which is largely due to the difficult transportation of oxygen to muscles and less active metabolism.

Women are generally more affected by the loss of iron in the system than men. Men are suggested to take around 9 grams each day, but women substantially increase that number to 15 grams each day. Menstruation is also a major cause of iron deficiency, so women with periods are implored to take more iron than men. If you are a vegetarian, it can be difficult to get all the iron you need since much of it comes from red meats. Iron supplements, then, are the best way for you to get the nutrients you need.

If you run frequently and for long distances, you may feel the strain of an iron deficiency in your diet. Some iron is lost when sweating, and other trace amounts are lost every day through the gastrointestinal tract, which makes increasing your supply extraordinarily important. If you are more interested in putting iron in your diet, add these foods to your list:

- Liver
- Kale
- Red meat
- Nuts
- Beans
- Dried fruit
- Dark poultry

Drink Water

There is an old saying regarding drinking water: "If you do not feel well, drink water; if you still do not feel well, you have not had enough." It may seem a little extreme, but the point is valid. Many people who suffer from dehydration feel nausea, stomach aches, headaches, and many other maladies. If you are feeling under the weather, grab a glass of water. Water makes up 50-60% of the body, and it powers a majority of the body's functions. Most processes in the cells depend on water to do anything, so a lack of water may cause you to feel sluggish.

Runners treasure water above any other substance. Marathon runners look forward to drinking from the water cups offered at the side of the road, keeping their bodies fresh and sustaining their demanding pace. Sweat is one of the primary causes of water loss in the body, and running for thirty minutes can cause you to lose 24oz of water. Sweating keeps the body cool during exertion, and a lack of water can cause sweating to stop altogether. Without a constant supply of water, the body cannot cope with the loss during long runs.

If you are new to running, begin the habit of drinking water consistently throughout the day. There is no prescribed formula for drinking, which means that you have to experiment with the amount you drink. However, as you are training, consistently increase the amount. You may feel a significant change in the way you feel after building the habit of drinking water often.

Pre-Run Meal

Though it is often up for discussion on how much you should eat before a run, the experts agree: you need to eat. Just as it is important to get all of the nutrients you need during the week from eating, so is it important to stock up on those nutrients before you hit the pavement.

Eating the night before a run is vital. This is the biggest meal before your exercise, but that does not mean you need to eat until you are about to burst. It is difficult to sleep when the stomach is full, which is another intricate part of the pre-run ritual. Instead, eat a meal that fulfills your nutritional requirements while giving yourself a little wiggle room, literally.

Now, runners eat in the morning, but this meal can be trickier. You do not want to overdo it right before a run; this can make you sick. Instead, eat small portions like toast or fruit. If you are eating before a race, you may be too nervous to eat large quantities anyway.

It's both possible and sometimes recommended to run on an empty stomach. Though this is far from the rule, you may feel better before heading outside without food acting as a weight in your stomach. Running on empty is usually only recommended for short distances, but that is open to interpretation. For example, if you are starting out, running one mile might seem like a long distance, but to someone who has been running for many years, five miles may be a short distance. The rule, though, is to provide your body with enough sustenance before a run. Treat your body with what it needs to succeed.

Post-Run Meal

Eating after a meal is vitally important. Unfortunately for many, running can cause a loss in appetite, making it difficult to remember to eat after a long run. However, your body needs helpful nutrients to recover from difficult work. After a run, stock up on carbohydrates and proteins and avoid white sugar. You need to increase your glucose levels, and proteins will aid in muscle recovery. And, as always, remember to drink water as part of your routine.

Chapter 3: Equipment

One of the most enjoyable parts of running is gearing up. There are so many different types of equipment to test out, it will hardly seem like a chore when heading out on the track. There are thousands of websites and stores that tell you what you need when you begin running, but they offer many differing views, and with so many options it can be overwhelming. When you begin running, it can be hard to choose among the many types of equipment, so this guide will help you sort out what you need and what you do not.

Shoes

Shoes are some of the most important equipment when it comes to running. After all, the high-impact nature of running often inflicts damage on feet that are not properly attired. The proper kinds of shoes can save both pain and money, so it is vitally important to choose the right shoes for your feet. Below are the best ways to choose the right shoe.

Choose a Running-Specific Shoe

Running shoes are highly specific to your feet. Think about the last time you put on a cheap pair of shoes. Not to mention the effect of wear over time, you likely slipped into a bad mood as soon as you slipped into shoes that did not fit properly or support the shape of your foot. It is a tale as old as time. Higher end running shoes are not only designed with you in mind, they are built to cradle your feet to specifications and stand the test of time.

Running shoes do just that, they help you run. Your feet will be protected from the high-impact nature of running while giving you a boost. These shoes are also intended to prevent injury. Little features, such as arch support, play a huge role in running both correctly and safely. But that does not mean you should go give the next shoe store clerk or website all of your money.

Choose the Right Fit

Even the most beautiful, high-end brand shoes can be an incredible waste of money if they do not fit you correctly. People with delicate arches may find that running without a shoe that supports the foot excruciating. When going to a store to find the right shoe, try to go in the afternoon or evening. Feet tend to expand as the day goes on, especially if you are on them all day.

Check where the shoe fits by placing a thumb between your big toe and the end of the shoe. You should have some wiggle room while you run, but only enough to run with a normal stride, and the sides should not pinch your feet. Though every shoe needs to be broken in, running shoes should feel very comfortable to your feet when you first try them on.

Choose the Right Type of Shoe

You want a shoe for running in, that is a given, but also consider what you will be using it for. If you plan to run long distances, find a shoe that holds up over long periods and is highly versatile. If you plan to do most of your running to and from the grocery store, you do not need a shoe that can take a constant pounding. Finally, trail running requires highly durable soles with a lot of grip. Find shoes that have deep tracks that allow you to stay on any surface regardless of its slipperiness.

Know the Value

Indeed, there are plenty of deals that can land you an excellent running shoe without putting out the big bucks. However, you will be paying top dollar for the right pair of shoes. A good pair of shoes usually run from $100 to $250, but they are built to last and you will get your money's worth.

If you choose to go the cheaper route, you may have to deal with the negative effects. Even when a shoe fits in the store you won't know the real value until they are tested. Out on the road you may experience not only foot pain, but back, shoulder, leg, and chest pain as well.

Know the Terminology

Stack height refers to the amount of shoe between your foot and the ground, and it is highly dependent on each person's preference. Some people prefer not to feel the ground when running while others like the more natural feel. Stack height is easily determined by comparing one shoe to another. Test out multiple types of shoes before settling on one. Remember that a larger stack height means a more cushioned run, and a lower stack height might mean that you can feel the pebbles beneath your feet.

Heel-toe drop refers to the amount of shoe under the heel versus the toe of the shoe. To find the right proportion for you, run briefly in bare feet. Notice how your feet land. If you put more weight on your heel when you run, look for a heel-toe drop that will allow you to move gracefully without putting too much pressure on one part of your foot. Most people run with a higher impact on their heels, so having a shoe with denser heel material is often the best way to protect your foot.

Protonation control determines how much your ankles twist when you run. If you are like the majority, your ankles will not roll much when running, so the average shoe on the market will work for you. However, some do encounter a greater proclivity to rolling ankles. In this case, you will have to find a specialized shoe to correct this issue.

Clothing

Running clothing is relatively easy to find, and there are many styles for many types of people, making it possible for each person to have a unique style. Aside from the generic "running clothes" label, there are many things to consider when picking out the right clothes for your run. Below is a list of things to consider when picking your next outfit.

Moisture-Wicking
When working out, it is inevitable that you will be covered in sweat. Sweat pooling on the skin is a breeding ground for bacteria and foul odor. That is where moisture-wicking comes in. The material for moisture wicking attire pulls the sweat from your body and moves it to the outside of the fabric where it evaporates.

Quick-Dry
Like moisture-wicking fabrics, this clothing allows your clothing to both breathe and keeps you from dripping sweat on the ground. Quick-dry fabrics are much more comfortable to wear when working out. Unless you want extra weight from your soaked t-shirt as you run and a closet that smells rank, it is best to keep the sweat-soaked clothes to a minimum.

Sun Protection
If you like to spend time outdoors, you should be conscious and find clothing that will protect you from the sun. Sunburns are not only painful, but they can cause other issues besides making running uncomfortable as the skin is less pliable when burnt. Though sunscreen should be your go-to whenever you step outside, if you plan to spend long hours outdoors—especially for long races such as marathons—wearing sun-protective clothing is your best bet. You are also less likely to

feel the intense heat if you find fabrics that are both breathable and UV light-resistant.

Thumbholes

Thumbholes in clothing are often a pain to deal with, especially if you have long arms, in which case thumb holes are misaligned and uncomfortable. However, if you can find jackets and long sleeve shirts with thumb holes, they can save you from having to buy running gloves or even wear gloves. Thumbholes keep sleeves in place during cold weather months, and they give you the benefit of knowing that you will not have to fuss with your sun resistant shirt or jacket during long runs.

Inner Liner

If you intend to spend a majority of your running career outside, finding clothing with inner liners is essential. They provide full coverage of your body and keep you warm without adding heavy layers. It is also helpful during other seasons to add to your comfort. Inner liners, especially in shorts will protect the body and are made from a soft fabric to avoid chafing. Constant friction can cause burns and the serious discomfort that follows if not appropriately attired.

Compression

Running is hard on the body especially when things are jiggling, but it doesn't have to be. To prevent discomfort, strain on muscles and other organs, invest in compression clothing to keep everything in place. Many stores sell leggings, shirts, underwear, socks, and shorts that will help you feel your best.

Utility

Find clothing that will allow you to carry whatever you need. Pockets are very important when running long distances (in case you need to stop to buy something or you just need to pack your cell phone for tunes). Choose jackets that are both aerodynamic and contain places to hold small and large objects.

Insulation

Insulated clothing is essential during winter months. Find clothing that traps heat and accommodates both your need for space while adding compression components. The best jackets are those that offer insulation without adding weight.

Chafe-Free Seams

Body parts rubbing is inevitable with high activity. Most athletic wear now offers chafe-free seams that prevent wear and tear from constant use and washing. Also, large bumps in clothing can irritate skin especially around the neck and under the armpit when it's beneath fabric. If this isn't an option for you, consider using deodorant. A slightly filmy deodorant applied to the skin will prevent chafing.

Mesh Vents

Many clothes now have mesh vents included. These are especially helpful in allowing your skin to breathe as you run. Mesh vents also allow for the easy evaporation of sweat once it soaks your clothing.

Reflectivity

Make sure that others can see you when you go out to pound the pavement. Many like to run at night because it is cooler and there are fewer people out, but this can cause a problem if you are not visible. To prevent accidents, invest in reflective gear that you can wear over or attach to your apparel. Many companies offer stick-on materials that easily attach to shoes or to the back of jackets to keep you safe when you are out on the road at night.

Fabrics

Polyester is one of the most common types of fabrics used for running. It can be used for compression or breathability, and it is commonly used for products like mesh tops and inner liners. Yoga pants and running leggings are made from materials such as lycra and nylon, and the technology continues to evolve the quality of the fabric all the time.

Merino wool, the name implies a heavy, itchy fabric but it is commonly used in quick dry and moisture-wicking products. It is designed for optimal breathability, making it ideal for serious workouts. Merino wool is known for its temperature regulation, allowing the body to maintain an optimal temperature.

What to Bring

Setting out for a run is not just about throwing on your favorite outfit and running shoes, especially when you have to consider the weather. Though there are many different extras you can bring with you on your run, try to keep the list down to a minimum, especially if you are running long distances. The clothing features listed above are just the beginning of what you should expect to wear when you head out the door.

Socks

When choosing socks to wear on a run, it is wise to choose materials that are not 100% cotton. Cotton does not always breathe well, as it traps sweat and makes it difficult to evaporate, leaving your feet wet. This is bad. The right sock provides moisture-wicking and enough padding to keep your feet as comfortable as possible. Running in socks that don't fit can cause blisters from your foot rubbing against the shoe. Socks that are comfortable are often the difference between a good run and a bad one.

The type of sock does not matter as much as the right material. Many people choose shorter socks in the summer and long socks in the winter, but this is not a hard and fast rule. Compression socks are highly breathable, so they can be worn year-round. But all of this depends on your personal preference.

Light-Weight Clothing

You will want to dress in layers when you are running in the winter, but too many layers can cause you to overheat, even in the coldest of temperatures. Dress for 20 degrees higher than what you plan to run in. For example, if you are running in 30-degree weather (Fahrenheit), then dress for 50 degrees. You will still have all the layers you need to keep you warm, but you will not become burdened with too many clothes and layers.

Sports Bra

If you are a woman, one of the most important parts of any running ensemble is a sports bra. Running without support can make muscles in your chest sag, and prolonged, rapid movement in the chest can cause upper and lower back pain. Running is a high-impact sport, so every step you take puts pressure on parts of your body that are not tied down.

Invest in a sports bra with a lot of support. There are many cheap alternatives available, but they won't provide the necessary comfort for running, so spending more money on a good athletic bra will pay for itself in the long run, especially if you have a large chest. Some women find it necessary to put on two sports bras to keep everything set in place. If you are still feeling the strain, put an exercise band around the top of your chest to keep the running motion down.

What Not to Bring

It's easy to make mistakes in running attire especially if you're hitting the pavement for the first time. Many mistakenly add unnecessary additions that not only weigh you down but will prevent you from running effectively. Below is a list of items to leave at home when you go for your next run.

100% Cotton

As previously discussed, clothing with 100% cotton is bad news if you want to maintain a comfortable body temperature. Cotton does not allow your body to breathe, and it can easily fall apart after regular high-impact workouts, leaving your clothing stretched out and useless. When you sweat, your clothes absorb all of the moisture and prevent you from performing your best. Cotton is also often the cause of chafing, which not only causes blisters but also causes holes.

Sweatpants

There may be a reason that sweatpants are more often used around the house than they are in the athletic arena. Sweatpants are made of cotton, which reinforces the reason not to wear them, but they are often bulky, making running long distances uncomfortable. Sweats are common winter attire, but they are not as effective as insulated gear now that do not carry the same bulkiness.

Sweatpants are also highly prone to nature. If you live in a region with high humidity, it will only be a matter of time before your sweats start to drift down because of the weight. If you like running on hiking trails, sweats pick up the dirt and moisture from the ground, keeping you filthy.

Worn Out Shoes

Perhaps one of the worst experiences is running with shoes that are worn down or past their prime. Shoes lose their shape and lose tread, so even though you may have found a pair you love, it is not worth it to constantly punish your feet if your shoes are not supporting you correctly.

Many experts suggest using more than one pair of shoes and trading each in after 250 miles. Of course, that is highly dependent on where you run. If you run through trails, you will likely need to replace your shoes more often as they become battered easily when running on uneven ground. When you notice your feet are blistering, aching or uncomfortable after a run, it's time and you will soon see the difference when out with a new pair.

Chapter 4: Warm-Ups

It is tempting to head right out the gate and go when you want to start running, but that can lead to consequences later. Just as running in the wrong kind of shoes can cause injury, so can running without warming up. Tendons, joints, and bones that are subject to the high-impact nature of running may still be limber enough without stretching, but you run the risk of jarring and bruising them, preventing you from running efficiently or safely.

If you have looked up any number of sites that offer suggestions for warm-ups, you will notice that there seems to be an endless supply of experts telling you to warm-up one way or another. There is nothing wrong with having multiple types of warm-ups, but you may not receive all of the same benefits you would by following a routine.

When you stretch your muscles, you force them to relax. Tight muscles contract and prevent the body from moving efficiently. Tight muscles also prevent the body from moving naturally. Muscles that are warmed up first are more elastic, letting the body spring back from impact. Consider a bowling ball and a basketball. The bowling ball is extremely rigid and resists any changes to its outside shell. When dropped, it thuds to the ground without bouncing. A basketball, on the other hand, has more elasticity. When it is dropped, it bounces back because it has a more flexible surface. The same principle applies to your muscles.

Warming up your muscles does just that: warms them up. The physical temperature change in your muscles after a warm-up makes them more able to contract and release easily. You may notice a slight burning sensation in your body as you stretch out muscles. This gets your muscles ready to contract and expand when exercising.

Warming up gets your nervous system ready for running. Without it, you may feel less able to accomplish running for long periods of time. This is because during warm-up, you are preparing your body for sensations it will experience during exercising. Track and cross country head coach at Columbia University Todd Weisse explained, "Without a warm-up that approximates the feel of the hard work you're about to do, you often cannot emotionally accomplish the workout well" (Lobby, 2018). If you have the choice between skipping the warm-up and running for longer or warming up and shortening your workout, choose to include the warm-up.

Your heart also benefits from a warm-up. Think about the last time you were woken up suddenly. You may have gotten out of bed, but you likely could not come out of a groggy, sleepy eyed phase for quite some time. The same kind of reaction happens with your heart. Warming up allows your heart to adjust to the high level activity and when the pumping in your heart speeds up, it increases blood flow to your limbs.

Warming up also helps build cartilage around your joints, allowing them to move smoothly. New studies have shown that even a little exercise (in which warming up does qualify) is enough to build extra cartilage. So, every time you warm-up before running, you are securing smooth movement between joints.

How to Warm-Up

Warming up isn't complicated; you don't have to search for new stretches or small exercises to help you start off. All you need is a set of movements that help you prepare each specific part of your body before you start running. Consider these tips to find the best warm-ups for you.

Muscle Focus

To start your warm-ups, consider which parts of the body you will use the most. Running, of course, is a whole-body exercise, so just stretching the legs is not enough. Perform both strength and stretching exercises to warm-up the muscles and get them ready for work.

Your arms play an enormous role while running, though it may seem like the legs do everything. Swinging your arms in such a way can cut down the energy expended in running by 3% to 13% when done properly. Consider running with your arms planted at your sides. Though you still get the job done, it is noticeably harder to run without a natural swing and it will feel awkward. Warming up the arms allows them to move easier as you run. You may see a remarkable difference in efficiency if your arms are prepared for running.

The legs are the powerhouses of this time span. They don't do everything, but the majority of running comes from the power below the belt. When you run, your quadricep muscles flex to move your leg forward and upward. As you extend, your hamstrings (which are the muscles extending from the back of the knee to the glutes) activates and forces your knee to bend. During this, the calf muscles stabilize your hips and feet and allow you to spring forward with every step. All of these muscles require stretching for the best results.

Your core, which are the muscles around the stomach and abdomen, provide your body the stability for running. The core is the center for all the limbs, making it the master of the rest of the body. Without a strong core, you will not be able to reach higher speeds nor maintain balance while running. If the core is engaged when running without a warm-up, it is not properly prepared for shifting in the body.

Maintain the Warm-Up

The effects of warming up don't last so doing so an hour before a run is not nearly as effective as warming up at the time of exercise. Consider the last time you did a simple chore like laundry. There are many bends and twists involved, and you may have felt the effects for a short while, but they faded quickly. The same applies to warming up before a run.

To keep your body warm if you are waiting to begin, continue to do stretches and short exercises until the time of the run. It is common to believe that if you continue to do exercises before you hit the pavement, you will run out of energy. However, when you stretch, you give your body the start it needs to complete the task. The more your blood flows, the more limber your body becomes and the easier it is to maintain that energy.

Short Race Equals Longer Warm-Up

If you just want to head out on a run for a few minutes, it seems strange to warm-up for longer. However, taking the time to warm-up longer saves your body from injury. Short runs are often faster and have larger impacts on the body while running, so the body takes a beating if it is not warmed up properly.

That said, your warm-up does not need to be half an hour to be effective. You need only to engage the muscles that you are going to use. Make sure there is blood flow to all limbs, avoiding any loss of circulation.

Start Slowly

In the same vein as longer warm-ups for shorter races, it is always important to start slowly. When many people stretch, they tend to bounce to get to touch their toes, stretch their arms, or stretch their hamstrings. This practice is not recommended, as it can lead to injury. Bouncing causes your body to force the muscles to relax at an accelerated rate, which could lead to pulled tendons and muscles. Before running, slowly perform your warm-ups to prevent injury.

Part of your run is also included in the warm-up. When you begin to run, your body is moving in a different way. This is the time to evaluate how your body feels. If you need to stop and examine parts of your body that are under strain, the beginning of the run is the time to do so. Running may not seem fun at first, but if you take care of the small aches and pains in the first mile of running, you will learn to enjoy it much more.

When you start slowly, you benefit from the growth of capillaries that bring more oxygen to your muscles. Starting right away can result in the growth of fewer capillaries and sacrificing some of these benefits. Take your time.

Starting slowly also leads to faster times overall. Though it may seem odd to think that a slow mile will get you a faster time, studies have shown that runners who start off slowly are often loose enough to finish the race at a quicker pace. Many take the story of the tortoise and the hare to mean that if you are prideful enough to take a nap during the middle of a race, you are bound to lose it. However, runners know that those who start out at their fastest pace lose energy quickly, making the nap almost seem necessary.

Reduce the Intensity

If you are breaking a good amount of sweat while warming up, you are putting too much effort in. Your body should not feel like it is experiencing a high intensity workout before you start to run. It is okay to break a sweat while warming up, but you should not feel your heart race elevated. If you are putting too much into it, slow everything down and take four deep breaths in through your mouth and out through your nose. By the end, you should feel less worked up.

Pre-Workout Warm-Ups

If you spend a lot of time searching the internet for running tips, you may notice that pre-workout and post-workout warm-ups are similar. For the most part, that is true. Both purposes are to warm muscles. However, pre-workouts differ because they focus on getting the heart rate up while stretching muscles.

If you are pressed for time, try to put in at least three minutes of warm-ups in your routine. You will see a change in your performance and efficiency if you warm-up as much as you can, but there are instances where long warm-ups just are not possible. When you can, do it for at least 10 minutes. Spend 45 seconds to one minute per exercise and give yourself at least 20 seconds of rest in between warm-ups. Below are several pre-workout warm-ups you can use for any running event.

Hip Flexor and Glute Leg Swing
One way to open up the body is to do a hip flexor and glute leg swing. This exercise opens up your hips and glutes, giving you a greater range of motion in your body.
1. Stand with your legs hip-width apart.
2. Stand on one leg and let the other swing in front of you like a pendulum, gently allowing it to swing for 30-45 seconds.

Walking Lunges
Lunges are an excellent exercise to get the legs and glutes warmed up. They also open up your hips by forcing your legs apart, forming a right angle.
1. Stand with your hands on your hips and your legs hip-width apart.
2. Place one foot approximately a foot and a half in front of you and bend at the knee, forming a 90-degree angle.

3. Sink into the bend until the foot beneath your hips lightly touches the ground.

4. Stand and walk the foot under the hips forward back to a standing position.

5. Continue lunges by walking forward, switching the initial foot every time, and repeat for 30-45 seconds.

Calf Raises

Because the calves are utilized so frequently in a running stance, it is important to warm them up to optimize their spring motions. The stretch compresses then releases the calf muscles, simulating high-impact movement.

1. Stand with the balls of your feet on the edge of a curb or stair with your heels unsupported over the edge.

2. Use the balls of your feet to lift the heels, tightening the calves.

3. Return to the original position to complete and repeat for 30-45 seconds.

Toe Dips

Perhaps one of the most common and painful maladies associated with running is the shin splint. At its most severe, it may feel as though the shin bone is cracking in half; at its least severe, it may feel like a pain in the shin that will not dissipate. To prevent shin splints, perform toe dips before every run.

1. Stand on a curb or stair with your heels on the edge and the rest of the foot dangling.

2. Move the toes down toward the ground and back up to complete a repetition.

3. Keep your back straight and hold onto a wall for support if necessary; repeat for 30-45 seconds.

High Knees

The high knees exercise simulates running but forces the body to raise the legs higher than average. This is a high-intensity training warm-up that is beneficial for the whole body.

    1.   Stand with your feet hip-width apart.

    2.   Simulate running, but pull your knees to at least waist-level and run in place for 30-45 seconds.

Butt Kicks

Like high knees, butt kicks simulate running, but this time targets the quadriceps and calves. However, this exercise is another warm-up for the whole body.

    1.   Stand with your feet hip-width apart.

    2.   Simulate running in place, but use your heels to kick your glutes for 30-45 seconds.

Marchers

Another great way to involve the entire body is through performing marches. These exercises use arms, legs, and core to stabilize and maintain posture while touching fingertips to toes.

    1.   Stand with your feet shoulder-width apart.

    2.   Keeping a straight-backed posture, lift the right leg to hip level, and touch your toes with your left hand.

    3.   Completing the move on both sides is one repetition; repeat for 30-45 seconds.

Jumping Jacks

Possibly one of the most classic types of warm-ups is the jumping jack. Children and adults alike use this method of exercise to get their heart rates up and warm-up all muscles in the body.

    1.   Stand with your legs hip-width apart and arms resting at your sides.

    2.   Jump and move your legs to the side while simultaneously raising your arms to clap above your head.

3. Jump back to the original position to complete one repetition; repeat for 30-45 seconds.

Arm Circles

Whether big or small, arm circles warm-up your arms, shoulders, and chest through repetitive motion. Moving in a repeated circular motion helps your body warm-up to the swinging arm motion of running.

1. Stand with your feet shoulder-width apart.
2. Bring arms directly up from your sides to form a T.
3. Circle arms in small circles and moderate speeds, gradually increasing size and reducing speed as the circles become larger; repeat for 30-45 seconds.

Walking

Perhaps the easiest of all warm-ups is walking. Walking provides a low-impact alternative to running that warms up your entire body. You do not have to be a speed walker to warm-up your body for a run. If you have the time, take a nice walk through the park to warm-up for a run.

Chapter 5: Running Techniques

When was the last time you felt a strain in your neck or stabbing pain in your side when you went running? Running for long distances often puts a lot of strain on the body, and those who are new to running often feel the brunt of that discomfort. However, this does not only affect newbies. Those who have been running for years can feel that pain as well when hitting the track. Pain is unfortunately common practice in running, but much of it can be avoided if you follow the correct running techniques.

As noted previously, running is a full-body workout. That means everything from your head to your toes is affected when you hit the pavement. Running with your arms swinging madly, tossing your body from side to side may seem like returning to the fun you experienced as a child, but it may cause more harm than good. If your body becomes accustomed to an improper technique, you may feel more pain as time goes on. Luckily, this chapter explains how to avoid it by focusing on your body from head to foot.

Head and Neck

Your head is surprisingly heavy. The average weight of a human head is around ten pounds, which can become a burden after some time if it is not properly positioned. If you are on your phone right now reading this book, take a moment to feel where your head is in relation to your body. Are you leaning forward as you read? Is your chin on your chest? Are you slumped over while reading the text? The rise of smartphones has caused many people to have bad head and neck posture, the leading cause of upper back pain.

Every square inch of your body is affected by air pressure. Since you live on this planet, you won't notice it. For an exercise, lift your arms in a T position, fingers reaching out. Hold the position for ten minutes. You will notice that the first minute is not difficult, but each subsequent minute puts more and more pressure on your arms, making them ache.

Now think of how this affects your head. Every square inch on your head is pulled down with approximately 15 pounds. Your body is designed to deal with this pressure by forming a relatively straight line from your head to your feet. In doing this, your body is exposed to the least amount of pressure possible. However, when your posture starts to slip, your body compensates for the adjusted burden, causing pain.

The neck is essentially a series of large muscles that hold up the head. When you lean your head forward, your neck strains to keep it up. Though the neck is incredibly powerful, it cannot do all of the work itself, especially when your head is pulled forward, so the upper back compensates. Many people develop a dowager's hump because they spend many hours every day looking down. To avoid the hump, keep your head squarely above your neck.

Leaning the head forward to look down also means that it is frequently close to touching the chest. Even if your head is not pushed forward, your neck still feels pressure from keeping your head in a stationary position. To avoid bad posture, place four fingers between your head and chest.

The same principles apply when you are running. When you stare at the ground while running, not only is air pressure forcing your neck to strain, but the jarring motions can also force your neck to work double time. Many people who experience upper back pain do so because of poor posture while running.

To avoid pain, keep your head directly above your neck and your chin parallel with the ground. When running on trails, it is almost impossible not to look down to avoid slipping in changes in the terrain. Maintain your posture, but use your eyes to view the trail from a distance.

Shoulders

Aching shoulders is another common malady that often affects most runners. When nervous or stressed, the shoulders naturally lift. Fear and excitement also cause the shoulders to rise, often causing knots to form. The body's natural response to tension during moments of stress is commonly manifested in the shoulders. In fact, check where your shoulders are right now. If they are raised, take a moment to roll them forward and backward to relieve any tension.

Though running has proven to aid in alleviating anxiety and depression, the natural tension of the body during running makes the shoulders creep up for those who do not know how to relax. The high-impact exercise often causes muscles in the body to respond by turning to a defensive position. The most natural form of defense is to bunch the body into the fetal position. Think about it. When your body is under attack, what does it naturally do? You bring your arms and legs up in defense of the most vital parts of your body, and that often means that the shoulders follow suit.

Shoulders also tend to bunch with poor posture. To compensate for the redistribution of weight, the shoulders tense and make the body better able to hold strong positions. The effects of always looking down at a phone translate to shoulders as well, so the body does what it does best: accommodate the changes.

To avoid shoulder pain, reach your chin to the sky for 10-20 seconds. Allow your body to readjust to proper posture and consciously tell your shoulders to relax. Once you lower your head, shake out your arms and let them swing from side to side while keeping your head in a straight-forward position. Perform shrugs and let your shoulders drop to their natural position.

When running, keep your shoulders back. To do this, roll your shoulders up then backward, letting them stop at a natural position behind your ears. Your shoulders should rarely move beyond your ears when you run. Since their natural position is in line with the rest of your body, they experience tension when they move either up or forward. Consciously make an effort to remain loose when running. Your body will accommodate your will as you run, and you will be infinitely more comfortable.

Arms and Hands

Just as with the shoulders, arms and hands tend to draw inward when they are under stress, causing tension. Many runners, both new and old, who experience this tend to leave their arms closer to their sides. Often, your hands ball into fists, and your arms stay at 90-degree angles that barely move. Not only does this become painful over time, but it also affects the way you run, ultimately hurting your running efficiency.

Arms that swing naturally give your body an extra boost when you hit the pavement. Consider the long jump. When athletes prepare to jump from a standing position, they move their arms back and forth in dramatic swings to gain enough momentum to propel their bodies forward. Your arms use the same principle when running. Each swing of the arm gives your body a little extra boost forward.

The natural swing of your arms also naturally reduces tension in your body. When your arms swing wildly, they prevent the shoulders from bunching. Of course, it is best to keep your arms from taking out your fellow runners, but your arms are some of your greatest allies when running, so it is wise to use them accordingly.

To improve your arm swing, bend your elbows at approximately 90 degrees and move them in only one direction, preventing them from swinging to the side. Use your shoulders to swing your arms. When you allow your shoulder to do much of the work, you simultaneously relieve tension in the shoulders and arms, allowing your body to move naturally. Also, relax your hands as you run. Your hands should close in light fists without letting them flap around. The tension in your hands can travel up your body if you are not careful.

Core

Your core is where most of your running comes from. When your arms and legs move, their motion is derived from the action of your core. The movement of your leg travels through your body to your core, which then responds by making your arms swing. All kinetic energy in running is derived from the strong muscles in your core.

Developing a strong core means fewer injuries on the track. Many who suffer from bad posture can experience injuries like back problems, muscle tension, and sprained ankles, among others. Because your core stabilizes you as you run, a tense torso that does not move often results in inflexible running. When you fail to twist and bend naturally, the rigidity in your body manifests itself in injury.

To improve your core performance, practice core-strengthening exercises such as planks, bends, and twists. Warming up is the first step to creating a flexible core, and many of the activities listed in the previous chapter warm-up your base and allow it to move naturally while you run.

Maintain good posture when you run. Tension in any part of the body affects the way your core performs. Tension in your shoulders prevents your core from twisting naturally, which often manifests itself in extra hip movement and pain. Tension in the hips forces the body to overcompensate for the lack of flexibility and also makes the back suffer. Pressure in the head prevents the rest of the body from moving naturally, as it attempts to correct the bad posture by tensing the shoulders and neck.

Imagine you are a puppet with a rope attached to the top of your head. When the puppeteer moves you from a sitting position to standing, you feel your body lift by the head, pulling you in a straight line. Keep this posture to avoid pain anywhere else in the body.

Glutes and Hips

As you run, you may notice your glutes play a large part in developing the right running posture, but pain can be experienced here due to a lack of proper movement. The glutes require activation before a run because they are what drive your legs forward. Weak glutes mean that you cannot achieve optimal motion when running, making them arguably the most important muscles when running.

A martial artist knows that one of the most important parts of learning to fight is to use your hips properly. The glutes are attached to the hips, allowing for smooth motion. When the glutes are not properly utilized, they prevent the hips from moving effectively, locking the lower part of your torso. If the lower torso cannot move naturally, the legs cannot reach full extension, causing you to lose momentum and express itself as back and hip pain. Runners often lack strong glute muscles because they use their back and legs more often, but improper posture makes running difficult.

When running, avoid hip drops. If you notice your hips move up and down individually, you are putting too much undue pressure on the rest of your body, often resulting in strong leg muscles but making you more prone to injury. Glute muscles have muscle memory, meaning they revert to whatever position is most comfortable. If you spend the majority of your time on the couch, your glutes can remain inactive while running. The only way to use your glutes to your advantage when running is to consciously stimulate them.

Before you start to run, perform exercises that will force your glutes to activate. Walking while paying strict attention to your hip movement is beneficial to learning glute activation. Also, perform known glute exercises such as squats or lunges, waking up the rest of your body as you make your hips and glutes move.

Thighs

Running is all about the legs. Though this myth is often perpetuated by non-runners, it does have a grain of truth. Your legs are essential to the process, and what holds them? Your thighs consist of the muscles between knee and hip, which include the hamstring and quads. When you see a professional runner, you can pick them out because of the size of their thighs.

The thighs are responsible for powering your legs forward. They are connected to the hips, which means that the strong muscles in your thighs are responsible for how far you can move your hips when you lift your leg, the muscles in your quadriceps, the muscles on top of your leg, contract. Lowering your leg and pushing off the ground while running is done by your hamstrings, the muscles located at the back of your legs. Each muscle dictates how far you can stretch your leg when you run, making the thighs responsible for setting the step size.

Many runners use their quadriceps as the primary muscles in their thighs. Though they are powerful muscles, too much dependence on them can cause injury. Instead, practice using your hamstrings as you run, pushing off with every step. The benefit is two-fold: you will put less weight on your quads, and you will redirect the much of the pressure onto the hamstrings and glutes, forcing your body to have better posture.

Tight thigh muscles also mean inefficient running. When your muscles are too tight, you cannot receive the full length of motion, preventing you from keeping proper posture. This may also affect your back, as the strain of the muscles shifts from your legs to your core. This is yet another reason to warm-up before running. Without them, running can become painful.

Think of how your legs move when running. Do your legs fan out both in front and behind you, or is most of the work done through only allowing your legs to reach under you before pulling them back up? Proper running posture is a pendulum-like swing of the legs with the center of your body as the midpoint. Consciously remind yourself to extend backward and straighten your back while running to maintain the right technique.

Dear reader,

I hope you are satisfied with your reading so far. If You haven't done it already, leave a short review; your opinion is important to me.

Peter Coleman

Knees

One of the most common injuries in the running world is knee injuries. The constant strike of the foot against a hard surface often makes knees tender, and improper form can lead to injury. Twisted knees often lead to broken cartilage and mutilated knees in the worst case. Therefore, it is crucial to keep an eye on your knees to make sure they are receiving proper care.

The knee is the part of the leg that forces your body to move forward. Though your hips and thighs instigate the movement, knee extension makes your legs pull you forward. Knees are primarily made of cartilage to allow for smooth movement. The kneecap is a bone that connects the ligaments and cartilage. After all, your knee is a joint.

To ensure you are maintaining proper posture, take conscious stock of your knees as you run. Note how your knees behave as you take simple movements forward. If your knees are prone to bowing, find corrective shoes that will help your knees stay healthy. Your warm-ups should also utilize the full range of motion of your knees. Try circling your knees for 30-45 seconds before each run. The low-impact motion of knee circling gives your knees the chance to move freely.

Many successful runners suggest running with a beat of around 180 strides per minute. Of course, that number is arbitrary based on how quickly you run, but the principle ensures that you maintain a good amount of steps while running. When you take shorter steps, you are not forcing your knees to propel you as far as long strides, which puts less stress on the knees in the long run. You can calculate your strides per minute by using a pedometer and a stopwatch.

Calves and Shins

Calf muscles are responsible for propelling you forward. Consider the calves as a place that puts a spring in your step. When your foot hits the ground, the calf muscles expand, absorbing the contact. When your foot leaves the field, the calf muscles contract, preparing you to leap forward to your next step.

Strong calf muscles come naturally to many runners, and as you continue to run, your calf muscles continue to increase in size. Since they are responsible for smoother, more natural motion, they are usually the first muscles to experience the jarring effects of running on a hard surface. However, they are also usually the first to experience pain when running improperly.

Shin splints are often common in the running world. Though the shin is the bone in your leg reaching from the ankle to the knee, it is not the only culprit for shin splints. The muscles, tendons, and bones around the calves become inflamed when experiencing shin splints, causing stabbing pains. The improper form that causes this is called dorsiflexion dysfunction.

Dorsiflexion refers to the movement the ankle makes when it makes contact with the ground. A large angle of dorsiflexion forces the toes toward the shin, and a short angle often looks like shuffling. Experts suggest that the maximum dorsiflexion for runners should be 15 degrees. Too much dorsiflexion causes floppy feet, which can cause injury and also be the source of shin splints.

Feet

Your feet are the breadwinners of the running body. They take the brunt of the punishment, and they are responsible for getting your body moving. The right amount of cushion could mean the difference between a healthy run and an aching foot. Even if you do not buy any other attire, invest in proper running shoes. Your body will thank you if you do.

However, there is more to running than simply letting your feet flop around as you move the rest of your muscles. There are many suggestions for proper foot posture when you are running, and much of it is dependent on what you find comfortable. A whopping 80% of runners choose to run heel-toe, about 15% run flat-footed, and the other 5% run toe-heel (Mitchell, 2018). Barefoot runners tend to strike with the middle of their feet and roll to the toes. Whatever your style of running, find the style that feels best.

Be careful when striking with any part of the foot. If you hit too hard or too often on one part of the foot, you may experience an injury. Focus on your footfalls when you run next and make sure that you are maintaining a healthy foot-strike method.

Chapter 6: Cool Downs

Since you have spent a reasonable amount of time warming up and running, why do you need to cool down? Can't you just stop and drink water or lay on the ground and ask: why do I do this? The answer is a resounding no! Cooling your body down gives it a chance to recuperate after an intense workout while simultaneously preventing injury. Yes, you can still injure yourself after you run. Cooling down becomes dramatically more important the longer you run.

After a run, the body is warm, and the heart will continue to beat at an exponential rate. These heart palpitations are normal after working hard, but it is important to make sure that the heart can calm down slowly. Your blood pressure also requires a chance to wind down. The body does not immediately stop pumping blood to your extremities when your run is complete. To prevent blood pooling, you need to continue moving. The heart can then adjust to the change in pressure and help your body relax safely.

The body creates lactic acid when running to compensate for the lack of oxygen entering the bloodstream. While this method allows the body to continue performing well, after a run, the lactic acid remains in your blood, causing soreness. If you immediately stop after running, the lactic acid does not have a chance to course through your system and dissipate in the body. Cooling down keeps your body in motion to prevent lactic acid buildup.

Cooling down also affects how quickly your body can heal itself. Because oxygen is required in the bloodstream, cooling down after a hard workout helps your body to repair any damages made while working out. Even if you have run for a long time, you still may experience small tears in the muscle that comes from pushing yourself. The cool down prevents your body from experiencing pain after this occurs.

It is common for legs to feel like wet noodles after completing a long run. After all, the body is not forcing the muscles to tense with each consecutive step. Since the muscles are still warm, they remain relatively relaxed unless stiffened by poor posture during the run. Cooling down stretches the muscles, usually producing better flexibility results than before the run.

How to Cool Down

For many, cooling down is the most fun of any run because it puts less pressure on the body and allows breathing to return to a normal rate. It is natural for the body to continue to feel the need to move after a long, difficult run, so cooling down immediately after a long workout should feel like a relief. Consider these tips to make the most out of your cool down.

Slow Then Stretch

There are two parts to a cool down: walking and stretching. Both are vitally important to lower your heart rate at a reasonable pace and to give your muscles the proper relaxation after working at a high level of intensity.

First, walk off your heart rate. Walk until your heart rate returns to normal, and you can return to normal breathing. When you advance in running, your threshold heart rate decreases because you have trained your body to accept high heart rates. The only way to increase your heart rate is to run further or faster. So, when you finish a run, the time it takes to cool down will vary depending on your level of fitness.

It is common for tension to build when you run. When you run for long periods, your muscles start to tighten from constant use. Therefore, the best time to stretch is right after a run. Stretching before a run is important, but you can get the most out of your stretches when your muscles are still warm.

Find the Right Pace

The cool down is supposed to calm your heart and allow you to breathe in slower, more regulated breaths. However, there is no prescribed pace in which to cool down. Experts suggest that the best cool down exercises are slower than the activities themselves. For example, if you choose to walk for a cool down period, you must walk at a pace slower than the pace at which you ran. Your body will still feel the effects of physical effort, but you are no longer putting undue stress on your body.

Many choose their cool down exercises to involve stretches or gentle movements. Light yoga is popular because it forces the body to stretch in directions in a more fluid motion than most standard stretches. It also forces you to breathe as you complete the forms, allowing your heart rate to slow and your body to acclimatize to the change in pace.

Run Barefoot

Though this is hardly a requirement, you may find that a light jog barefoot might help circulation in your body. Running shoes are essential for running correctly and cushioning the blow when your feet strike the ground. However, when your toes are bunched inside shoes for a long time, they may start to feel uncomfortable. Running barefoot gives you the freedom to run without toes splayed allowing muscles in your feet to spread without resistance.

Get a Massage

This is the time in your routine that requires some of the most attention. Your body is relaxing after a long period of hard work. So, take the time to get a massage. You do not have to go to a professional masseuse to improve your recovery time, either. Use a roller to stretch out your muscles, and put pressure on the areas that are the most sore. Remember, you should not feel pain when using a roller, only discomfort. It may take some time before your muscles fully relax, so enjoy the time and go slowly.

Also, practice self-massage. Plantar fasciitis is a common malady for runners, as they spend a majority of their time on their feet. Plantar fasciitis occurs when the tissues at the bottom of your heel become inflamed, causing pain. Gently massage the area, taking care not to press too hard. This inconvenience can become especially difficult when you run regularly. Let your heel heal naturally by giving it a good rub.

Protein Shakes

Treat yourself to a protein shake after running. Protein builds muscle and helps your body alleviate soreness, so it is important to get the right amount of protein into your system. Your body is most receptive to nutrients after working out, so it is important to consume protein shakes within two hours of completing your workout.

Hydrate

If you remember nothing else, remember that it is vitally important to hydrate. You are made up of nearly 70% water, and when your supplies become low, you can experience some unpleasant side effects like headaches and stomach aches. Water is also responsible for removing lactic acid from your system, which builds up when running and causes soreness. So, immediately after working out, grab at least two glasses of water to wash down the excess lactic acid buildup.

It is important to drink water throughout the day, so drinking water after a workout should be a part of every cool down session. Even if you do not feel like drinking, drink. Part of weight loss is water which comes out as urine, sweat, and tears (if you are really struggling with running). The water you consume will not only make your body feel better after a workout, but throughout the rest of the day as well.

Post-Workout Cool Downs

Cool downs can be some of the most fun experiences when running. After all, you have just finished your run, and now you can let your body stretch without fear of injury. You can also explore new cool downs that will help you depending on the type of running you perform: interval and short distances or long distances.

Cool downs are about making your body relax and return to normal after a high-impact exercise, so their effectiveness is dependent on how much effort you put into them. If you have short cool downs or skip them altogether, you will experience soreness and possibly pain due to your body's quick transition. Below are some exercises to consider when cooling down.

Walking
The first cool down exercise is walking. After a run, let your body cool down by slowly decreasing your pace as you walk. Take deep breaths in through your nose and out through your mouth to regulate your breathing. As you walk, allow your arms to swing freely and rotate your neck. For the best results, walk for 1-5 minutes after your run.

Low Lunge
The low lunge stretches out your hips, spine, and chest. This yoga pose gently forces your body to extend your quads as you stretch, also providing your back with much-needed movement after a run.

1. Lower your body into a high plank position.
2. Place one foot in between your hands and lower your opposite leg's knee to the floor.
3. Keep your back straight as you raise your hands to the sky.

4. With your hands still straight over your head, gently start to pull them toward your back foot to stretch out your spine.

5. Once you have reached a position that is uncomfortable but not painful, hold the position for 30-45 seconds.

Half Split

This stretch targets your calves and hamstrings while you remain in a kneeling position. Because the hamstrings and calves are often tight after a run, consciously force your muscles to relax to get the most out of this stretch.

1. Stand with your feet hip width apart.

2. Place on foot approximately 1-2 feet in front of you.

3. Flex your ankle so your toes are as close to your shin bone as possible and bend the knee of your standing leg.

4. Bend forward to reach for your toes while keeping your back straight.

5. If you are not getting enough of a stretch, kneel on one leg and stretch the other leg in front of you. For an even more advanced move, perform a side split; perform for at least 30-45 seconds.

Wide-Leg Forward Fold

This all-inclusive move stretches your calves, hamstrings, neck, outer ankles, and back with one move. Since you are working to gently stretch your muscles, do not bounce as you bend forward.

1. Stand with your legs spread as far as they will go without strain, feet facing forward.

2. Slowly bend forward while keeping your back straight; hold this position for at least 30-45 seconds.

Warrior Pose III

If you are unfamiliar with yoga and do not know how to do this move, go slow to work on maintaining balance. This stretch works your abdomen, arms, back, neck, hamstrings, calves, and feet.

1. Stand with your feet hip-width apart.
2. Reach your hands above your head, reaching your fingertips as far as they will go.
3. Standing only on one leg and keeping your back and arms in a straight line, move your arms to point your fingers in front of you, your other leg acting as the other end of a bar and coming up straight behind you.
4. Stand on one leg and balance in this position for 30-45 seconds.
5. If you are having problems maintaining balance, you may allow your other foot to lightly touch the floor; repeat on both sides.

Garland Pose

Squats are highly beneficial to your glutes, hamstrings, and quads, and staying in a squatting position allows your body to balance as you force your muscles to relax. This move may feel uncomfortable for those who are not as flexible or used to putting so much weight on your feet while maintaining balance. You may adjust this pose slightly to make it more comfortable by not sinking into a full squat.

1. Stand with your feet shoulder-width apart and turned outward slightly.
2. While keeping the heels and balls of your feet planted on the ground, sink down into a squat so your butt comes as close to your heels as possible.
3. Place your elbows on the inside of your legs and put your hands together in a pose.
4. Stretch your hips by forcing your elbows upward and your legs apart; hold this position for 30-45 seconds.

Standing Quad Stretch

Perhaps one of the best-known stretches is the standing quad stretch. Since your quads take a beating when running, the quad stretch allows your large leg muscle to relax as you stand. If you are not comfortable about your balance, use a wall to push on during the stretch.

1. Stand with your legs hip-width apart.
2. Flex your ankle so your toes reach toward your shin and pull one leg behind you with both hands.
3. Attempt to get the heel of your foot to your butt while pulling your leg toward the center line of your body.

Butterflies

This stretch is named after a butterfly because the legs form a butterfly position when you sit on the ground. This move stretches out your hips and inner thighs.

1. Sit on the ground with a straight back.
2. Put the bases of your feet together and pull them to your body until you are uncomfortable but not in pain.
3. For more of a stretch, try to touch your belly button to your toes; hold this position for 30-45 seconds.

Standing Calf Stretch

This simple exercise gets the blood flowing in the calves while letting your calf stretches naturally. This stretch prevents soreness in calves and gives you extra mobility next time you run.

1. Stand with your feet hip-width apart.
2. Extend one foot in front of you, pulling your toes as far back toward your shin as possible.
3. For a better stretch, bend forward slightly until you are uncomfortable but not not painful; hold this position for 30-45 seconds.

Chapter 7: Fatigue

Fatigue, a constant enemy to all runners, or is it? Fatigue is the feeling of excessive tiredness, especially after training for long periods of time. Though your body does not shut down, your limbs seem to feel like rocks. Even if you have been getting enough sleep at night, it is possible to feel fatigue in your muscles, making it difficult to continue running.

Fatigue is caused by the body's excessive use of one muscle. For example, imagine going to the gym every day to lift weights and improve your biceps. Though you may feel great for the first few days, soon the burden of exercising one muscle every day starts to wear on your body, even if you are using the weights properly. Runners experience fatigue in their legs, backs, cores, and arms often because of the repetitive nature of the sport. The same muscles are worked every day, making them tire quickly.

It is for this reason that many people change their styles of running or do other cardio to get the most out of their workouts. When lifting weights on off days, runners tire other aspects of their bodies, giving muscles that suffer from repetitive motion a rest. Though the muscles still tend to tire over time, they won't as fast.

One of the most important parts of training is learning how to deal with fatigue. Sometimes training becomes too intense, and you must take a step back to make the most out of your running. However, there is something to be said about fatigue's ability to help you run more effectively in the future.

Why Fatigue is Important

When training, the body reconstructs as the muscles adapt to the changes in exercise. The muscles tear when exposed to stress and build again, but stronger, allowing your body to work harder the next time you train. The tearing and reconstruction of muscles often means that the body becomes sore after a difficult training session. Often, this means that the muscles are not able to produce the same amount of force when pushing off to make you go faster. Essentially, you feel like you are putting in more work for the same results.

However, after the muscles are reconstructed, they experience a rise in efficiency: They are built stronger than before. This is the primary way runners and all muscle builders benefit from fatigue. The rise in efficiency takes time and often feels as though you are losing progress, not gaining it. However, taking care of your body and training at the right times can make muscle growth work for you.

While many want to see results right away, physical change won't happen that fast. This is why runners have rest days because running full speed every day does not help you improve either pace or distance. It may only take a day for your muscles to heal completely, but it is more likely that your muscles will take a few days, even up to two weeks, to fully recover.

This does not mean that you should stop running for two weeks at a time. Far from it. In fact, you should be spending that time building up your muscles in other ways. Taking frequent walks and working out at slower paces keeps your body active without tearing muscles to injury. Drinking water and stretching before and after workouts also gives your body time to rest and will speed up the healing process.

Studies have shown that accumulated fatigue, the results of fatigue in the body for long periods of time and over many workouts, can actually help you improve your training speed and distance. Muscles that tear need time to heal themselves before returning in a stronger form. If you continue to train even when you are sore, more muscles will tear, causing more fatigue. Pushing your body when it is fatigued gives your muscles more chance to recover in greater quantities.

Say you do a HIIT workout with many squats and lunges, causing your muscles to tear. The next day, you continue to train, and your muscles do not feel as strong as they were the day before. However, you continue to train, finally allowing yourself 2 days of rest after five days of consecutive work. It may feel as though you have irreparably damaged your legs or your body cannot take any more stress. You were doing the same number of repetitions every day, so your muscles never got a break.

During those two days, your muscles start to knit together. Instead of damaging your legs, however, the time you spent training your legs resulted in muscles that were stronger than before. Each tear built upon itself to create stronger muscles than before.

The same applies to running. Though you are not performing specific weight exercises, you are using your body weight as your feet pound the pavement. The more you weigh, the more your body endures, so someone who weighs 250 pounds may need to run shorter distances than someone who weighs 150 pounds because the force required to lift the 250 pound person's weight off the ground is much higher. Do not be fooled into thinking that you are getting less of a workout if you weigh more. Sometimes starting slowly is the best way to get your muscles acclimatized to running.

Be careful, not to train too often. If you continually subject muscles to the same stress every day, they begin to weaken significantly over time. You need to find a balance between training and rest. Make sure your rest days still involve some form of exercise. Run at a slower pace than your regular training schedule, or find a low-impact form of exercise that will allow your muscles to heal as you continue to work.

Taking additional breaks every five to six weeks is also highly beneficial to your body as it allows accumulated fatigue to subside. You can still work out on your days off, but they should only be at 65% power of the training pace. Remember that, when you take a week-long break with no intense exercise, you will not lose the muscle you have gained. It takes at least two weeks to see even a slightly noticeable change in pace or power. You are responsible for keeping your body happy, so make sure that you give it time to rest when needed.

Reasons for Muscle and Training Fatigue

Though it is obvious that training fatigue is frequently caused by working your muscles too hard, that is not the only explanation. In fact, if you are facing a continuous barrage of fatigue after carefully selecting your route and training method, there may be something else at work that prohibits you from performing to your highest capacity.

Overtraining

Often runners believe that they will feel fatigue after every run. Though that is true for some cases, running in and of itself should not make you feel tired or overworked unless you are doing too much. This can manifest when you bite off more than you can chew in the training department.

Instead of choosing a running program that is best for the body, runners make the mistake of choosing a course that they believe they might be able to handle. If you have never run in your life, it is no surprise if you break down at some point during a marathon. Many runners see other people's goals and believe that they are not doing enough if they are not living up to those standards. Social media paints the joyous portions of a run, but it fails to portray the hard work, dedication and aching muscles that go along with it. Do not assume that you can work hard as the pros without suffering from muscle fatigue.

Runners who are training for long distance races also tend to push their bodies too far, even those who have been running for years. It is common to feel as though you can make that last mile if you just put in more effort and push yourself, even if your legs are aching. Runners that feel they are behind in

101

preparation often push themselves too far, causing injury and forcing them to rest for months instead of days.

Fatigue from overtraining is only cured by taking the time to let your body rest. Muscles that are pushed too far may ache for days, making it difficult to perform basic tasks. Take ample time in your schedule to let your body adjust to changes in training and allow your body to rest.

Training by Pace

Many new runners feel like breathing is a chore for the first few days of active running, so it is less common for them to suffer from training by pace. However, as the days progress, it is more likely that their fatigue is caused by training at faster paces. Many feel the pain of not reaching the same pace that they used to achieve in the years they were more fit, so they push their bodies to the limit.

The most common form of this occurs when training for a race or other competition. Runners believe that they need to increase their pace so that they can qualify for a more advanced group of racers or increase their positions in a competition. Though gradually increasing your speed as you train is an ideal form of improvement, many push too hard and either cause too many micro tears in their muscles or they do not receive the physical rest necessary to accommodate the new exercise.

Training should primarily focus on strengthening your body. The muscles that you gain while you train are developed at a rate that is comfortable for your body when you train at an average pace. The body naturally adapts to the change in exercise by changing aspects as you continue to train. When you run, you should focus on what your body can achieve, not what you believe it should.

One of the most difficult lessons for new runners is to cater your life to your body, not the other way around. Instead of pushing your body beyond what it is capable of, listen to how your body responds when you apply new stimuli. When you run, focus on the energy you receive from your body and gently increase your speed as you continue to train, always promoting discomfort instead of pain.

Lack of Sleep

Sleep plays a major role not only on the body, but also on the brain. Though exercising may not always determine how well you sleep, how well you sleep is essential to understanding why you feel training fatigue. The more sleep you get, the more chance your body has to heal and improve with each session.

When the body does not receive enough sleep, it starts to turn on itself to make up for the recovery. Sickness and mental problems can pop up during sleep deprivation. Anxiety and depression are common ailments to people who do not sleep enough, and the state of your mental health plays a large role in the success of your training. Fear and lack of motivation are common illnesses that beat the joy of running out of you.

Marathon runners sleep a whopping 10-12 hours every day and sometimes include a nap. Why? They need that time to recover from the incredible training program they perform each day. Sleep is nature's drug to take care of your body. That is the reason that the sick are told to sleep as much as they can. The body repairs itself during sleep and rejuvenates the body better than any drug on the market.

If you are new to running, you may feel the need to sleep more than you originally do because of the extra stress on your body. Plan wisely and do not let sleep overcome you as you begin to train. Too much sleep is also problematic

Unhealthy Eating

If your body is not getting the nourishment it needs to complete difficult tasks, it will not perform up to standard. Sugars, salts, and excess fats are often the culprit for fatigue and inability to maintain a pace that suits your training program. Though the body may be receiving enough nutrients from other sources of food and supplements, foods that are not healthy have a tendency to weigh you down.

It is also possible to suffer from insufficient calorie consumption. Though many runners eat more than those who are not as active, they burn calories at a greater rate, which means that many do not eat enough. For example, protein is very important to runners, but some skimp on the protein to eat more carbs. Though they are getting the right caloric amount, they are not eating the right kinds of foods.

To fix this problem when starting out, remember what you are eating with a food journal. This will help you get the right caloric amount without sacrificing any vitamins, proteins, fats, carbs, and proteins you need to keep a well-balanced runner's diet. Though the suggested ratio is 60% carbs, 15% protein, and 5% fat, you may feel comfortable with a different arrangement. As long as your body is content with the amount of nutrients you receive, keep the diet you have.

Stress

One of the most difficult forms of fatigue to overcome is stress. When the body is constantly in a state of stress, the body remains in a highly tense condition, causing heart palpitation and muscle soreness. Raising the shoulders is a common indicator of stress. This plays a significantly negative role on your muscles, causing fatigue. Shoulders play a major part in running, keeping the arms swinging naturally and propelling the body forward. With sore muscles, the body cannot behave in this way, and the running form has to pick up the slack.

Experiencing continual stress is often a sign of anxiety, a mental illness that perpetually keeps the body in a state of fight-or-flight. Remaining in this mindset makes muscles increasingly sore over time causing problems like chronic back pain or poor circulation. Though running can help overcome some types of anxiety, if the body has remained in a heightened state of fear for long periods, fatigue sets in easier.

To combat stress, keep a journal of your thoughts and use running and sleeping as a resource to reduce the muscle tension in the body. Develop motivation to run, and maintaining a healthy schedule of running will help you overcome anxiety. When the adrenaline stops flowing throughout the body, it can finally relax, allowing you to run further and train harder.

Overcoming Training and Muscle Fatigue

Training and muscle fatigue forces the body to slow down, preventing you from working harder toward your goals. While a little is beneficial, overwhelming fatigue can be harmful to your health. To make sure that you are getting the most out of your training program, consider these tips to rid yourself of training and muscle fatigue.

Eat and Drink Often

Make sure that your body is fully prepared for training by eating and drinking water often. While food is your fuel, water is your lubricant and helps your body function in a changing program. Follow the nutrition guide in Chapter 2 to help your body acclimatize to proper training techniques and rigorous exercise.

Many diets tell you to eat anything you want as long as it is below a certain amount of calories. Though that advice does help you lose or maintain weight, it does not help you get the most out of your diet. Eating fruits gives you natural sugars and carbs, which produces energy in the morning and throughout the day. Eating protein in the morning and after a workout helps your muscles work and heal properly. Starches and other carbs give you the temporary energy you need to power through any workout. Experiment with your diet to find out which works best for you.

Water is the key to life. Though the body can survive more than a week without food, it requires water to prevent organ failure. Plan how much water you plan to drink before the day begins and reward yourself once you have reached that threshold. The more water you drink, the better you will feel.

Shorten Your Stride

Not only is it important to slow down to reduce muscle fatigue while training, but shortening your strides prevents your body from experiencing high impact when your feet hit the trail. You still get a good workout from shortening your stride, but your joints and muscles do not take as much punishment. Shorter strides require less muscle extension as well, which means that your muscles do not have to work as hard to do the work, effectively giving your body a break after micro-tears.

Practice raising your knees higher as you run. When you run in a skating motion, your body does not distribute blood as effectively as when you force your muscles to propel you higher. Also, raising your legs higher as you run helps you climb hills more effectively. Your body uses the raising of the legs to propel the body up with greater ease.

Listen to Your Body

This advice has circulated throughout the book, and for a good reason. Though this book gives you the right information to ensure your body can handle difficult transitions into running, it is ultimately your body that calls the shots. If you feel you need to run slow one day and save a fast run for another day, do so.

Change Your Focus

Running consistently is difficult. It takes a lot of practice, and skipping a week can feel like a death sentence for your running career if you lose your motivation. Aching legs while running is also a difficult thing to ignore, but with time it is possible. Sometimes all you need to do is find a new point of view. Pain is relative. The body experiences pain because receptors in the body send a signal to the brain to feel discomfort. A way to get rid of pain is by imagining something else.

Of course, this is easier said than done. The pain you feel in your body tells your brain to focus on it over nearly everything else. However, the key to changing your focus is to find an outside motivation. Some people listen to music or an audiobook while running to forget the pain and continue to run. As long as you do not focus on it, you need not feel any pain.

Remember, however, to know the difference between discomfort and pain. Pain is the body's way of telling you that something needs to change. Pain alerts you to injuries and ignoring it could be detrimental to your health. Allow your motivation to push you to train harder, but do not let it overlook your feelings of pain.

Chapter 8: Injuries and Prevention

Perhaps the bane of any athlete's existence is injury. Pain from an injury is not just isolated to the injured region but the brain as well. Sprained ankles and pulled muscles can put runners up for weeks at a time, preventing them from using the body they have specially molded to train. Anxiety and depression can follow injuries that take more than two weeks to heal, which leads many into a downward spiral, sometimes avoiding activity from fear of aggravating the injury.

If you have been injured while running and experience this fear, take comfort in knowing that you are not alone. A study conducted in 2017 for the National Running Survey determined that 75% of runners confirmed that they had been injured in the last year, and half of those had received an injury that took more than four days to heal (Abbate, 2019). The highly popular sport, though beneficial to health, causes injuries if you are not careful.

Running has several injury risks that prevent participants from staying on the road every year. Some of the most common injuries include runner's knee, hamstring pulls, shin splints, piriformis syndrome, and Achilles tendonitis, but each of these comes with a grain of hope: there are ways to prevent these injuries.

Runner's Knee

Many people use the term "runner's knee" as a blanket term for anything that happens to your knees when running. It is common to feel pain on the knee, or in and around the kneecap. Runner's knee can get worse as you go up or downhill and is sometimes accompanied by a sharp popping noise. If it becomes too bad, the knee sometimes swells, making it difficult to run.

It is common to experience a runner's knee when adding miles to a training program. Some runners feel the need to add miles quickly without listening to their bodies because they want to increase time, or they don't want to fall behind. The knee becomes gradually worse when runners do not take time off for it to recover and run through the pain.

Runner's knee is caused by improper form and is often the result of poor core strength. With the increase of miles, runners often do not recognize that they are running poorly, putting more pressure on their knees as they go. Imbalances in the knee take over the rest of the body and soon you may start to experience pain in other areas like the hips and back, as runners often try to alleviate the pain by deferring it to other portions of the body.

Runner's knee is often the result of extended time in poor form, as most won't recognize it at first. For this reason, runner's knee can seem like a sudden onset, something that should have manifested itself right away but was delayed due to increased stress.

Prevention

One way to prevent runner's knee is to find the right shoes. Yes, it always comes back to the shoes. When you run with shoes that do not support your feet, the rest of your body suffers. Shoes that do not keep your feet in an upright position will put pressure on your knees as you run, and those whose

110

ankles bend slightly inward or outward when running also cause undue stress on parts of the knee.

Work out other parts of your body. Runner's knee is a common symptom of weak core muscles. The core keeps the body upright, and when the body does not maintain proper posture, knees can bend inward or outward, causing pain on either side of the knee. Too much stress on the knees can damage cartilage, which may result in more serious injuries.

Perform eccentric weight training to get your knees used to the changes in pressure during running. Weight training allows your knees to gain strength in a controlled environment, and mixing weight training with your running routine will help your body adapt quickly to schedule changes. Exercises such as squats are perfect for knee strength as they force the body to maintain balance as your butt lowers to the ground.

Treatment

If you do fall victim to runner's knee, there are ways to treat the injury that will help you back on your feet. The first step is to address the pain you feel when you run. Without acknowledging the pain you feel, it is difficult to diagnose and treat. Once you have recognized the spots that experience the most pain, give your body the rest it needs to recover.

Icing your knee is a great way to reduce swelling. If you notice that your knee tends to pop frequently and often feels warm and inflamed after running, stop your program immediately. It is important not to aggravate the injury more. Repetition of applying ice to your injury allows it to heal sooner. Use a cloth or other fabric barrier to prevent the cold from causing your muscles to tighten. Hold the cloth of ice over the injured knee for 20 minutes at a time, six to eight times every day.

Another way to reduce swelling is to add compression. Use a wrap to compress your knee and elevate it to prevent blood from pooling down at your feet. Keep your knee at a slight bend to prevent it from stiffening as you relax it. If you have chronic pain, consult a doctor to get more advanced treatment.

Hamstring Pull

A pull in the hamstring can feel like a sharp pain in the back of the leg, especially when you sit or extend your leg. Hamstrings are commonly pulled due to improper warm-ups and cool downs from the previous run. When you fail to cool down after a run, your body becomes rigid, and it often does not relax properly. This leads to hamstring pulls. Hamstring pulls also occur when excess weight is applied to the leg, which often indicates poor running form.

Hamstring pulls can keep a runner down for a few days to even a few weeks, and it is extremely easy to pull again if you do not follow proper warm-up and cool down techniques or run properly. It is common to pull a hamstring while running because the body is put under stress to perform quickly, and the hamstring may not be warmed up enough to account for the excess strain of stretching the muscle.

Prevention
The best way to make sure that your hamstrings will be prepared for your next run is to exercise and strengthen the area. Many runners use weight lifting as a method to prevent injury this way. With more muscle, the hamstrings are better able to cope with high-impact behavior, making running both easier to perform and safer from injury.

When you begin to run, start off slowly. Even after a warm-up, muscles are not able to handle the rapid change in stress when running at high speeds. Experts recommend that your first mile should be slow with reasonable stride lengths. Athletes who run short distances quickly often suffer from hamstring pulls if they do not spend at least ten minutes, allowing the muscles to contract and expand safely.

If you have previously injured your hamstrings, be extremely careful the next time you run. 60% of runners who have pulled a hamstring in the past experience it again (Abbate,

2019). The body is remarkable in its healing, but it does need help from you. The best way to determine if you are going to pull a hamstring again is to listen to your body and determine if your muscles are too fatigued to continue.

Treatment

If you receive a hamstring injury, stop running immediately. That will only aggravate the injury, making it more difficult to heal. When a hamstring is pulled, it is common to feel as though your leg will not fully extend. Do not push your body by forcing it to do so. If you can, sit on the ground or call a friend to pick you up. While it is possible to continue walking on your leg after it has been injured, doing so will only result in more pain.

Pulling a muscle causes it to become inflamed. It is not uncommon to see swelling after pulling your hamstring badly. Applying ice will reduce the swelling and help your body relieve the pain naturally. If the injury is very bad, use pain killers while you gently ice your leg. Do not force your leg upward, pulling the muscle further.

Use a foam roller to release the tension in your muscles gently. Foam rollers come in many different styles; some are round, and others have ridges to help you knead the muscles. Whichever you choose is up to you, and its effectiveness is simply a matter of preference. Do not force your body to relieve tension quickly by putting all your weight onto the roller. Gently massage the area to increase blood flow and improve feeling.

Some hamstring pulls are bad enough to require up to eight weeks of healing time. That may seem like an eternity for a runner, but there are ways to run with a pulled hamstring. Use compression to prevent your hamstring from overextending while you run and take shorter strides. As long as you do not push your workout, your hamstring will hold up.

Shin Splints

Shin splints are the bruising of bones, tendons, and muscles in the leg between the knee and foot. The bruising puts pressure on the bones and muscles, often causing inflammation and discomfort. Shin splints can feel like a slight discomfort in the shin bone area, or it can feel like your shin is splitting in half. One of the most uncomfortable injuries to experience is a shin splint in the middle of a race. Many experience shin splints that are so bad that they have to stop running immediately. The injury can extend from the arches of the feet to the knee in severe cases.

However, shin splints are usually not as serious as other injuries, and they heal quickly given rest. Shin splints are common to new runners who are not used to the stressors running puts on the body. The high-impact nature of running puts incredible pressure on shins and calves, and those who are not used to it can feel the pain for a few days to weaker symptoms the following week.

If you experience chronic pain, it may lead to something more serious. Fractures can often feel like shin splints during running, and no amount of ice will fix that if you do not let it rest. Before you self-diagnose yourself, be sure to check with a physician who can tell you if your shin bone has a fracture.

Prevention
The best way to prevent shin splints is with the right pair of shoes. New runners who do not have enough cushion in their shoes start to feel the pain quickly, especially if they naturally extend their legs further than others. The pain usually occurs when landing incorrectly on the feet, causing them to receive a more jarring effect. Find a pair of shoes that will hold your feet in the right positions as you run, and redistribute your weight as your feet hit the pavement.

Another preventative measure is to shorten the length of your strides. If you are new to running, keep your feet close to each other as you run. You can also practice on low-impact machines like ellipticals to build up your resistance to the high-impact nature of running.

Treatment

The first step to take is to stop moving. More stress on shin splints will make them ache and bruise more. If the bones, tendons, or muscles become more inflamed, it can feel difficult to walk. Rest your legs for a few weeks to make sure that everything is in order before you start to run again.

Ice is the go-to treatment for many injuries because it helps reduce inflammation, and this is once again an answer to shin splint treatment. Some shin splints are so painful that they require rubbing ice against the skin to improve circulation. If your shin splints become chronic, you will have to adjust how you are running and see a physical therapist to make sure that you are running correctly to avoid injury.

Piriformis Syndrome

Piriformis syndrome refers to the pain felt in the buttocks when the sciatic nerve is pinched during running. The piriformis muscle is located on the small of the back and connects the lowest vertebra to the muscles and bones in the legs. In this "notch" where the two bones meet, the sciatic nerve can become pinched, causing pain in the gluteal region.

This issue is most common in women, though there is not enough research to understand why this is the case. An estimated 5% of runners have experienced this pain in their running careers (Shmerling, 2018). If you are experiencing chronic lower back pain, be sure to check with a physician to make sure you do not have piriformis syndrome.

When many feel the pain, they believe it is related to lower back issues or pulled muscles in the glutes. Pain starts in this region but often travels downward on the bottom half of the leg--including the hamstrings and calves--and may extend to the feet. It is also common to feel that you cannot sit on one side of your buttocks.

Because every diagnosis is based on clinical results, which refer to symptoms only and no external tests, it is not always certain how common the syndrome occurs. It is possible to mistake piriformis syndrome as a slipped disc, and further inspection is needed to determine if this is correct. There is also no certain way to determine how long it will last, so when running, you have to take it by ear.

Prevention
Since piriformis syndrome relates to a pinched sciatic nerve, there is no definitive way to prevent the occurrence. However, building muscles in your back, core, and legs may help. Muscles that are better able to handle keeping the body upright are more likely to prevent piriformis syndrome.

Treatment

The mainstream ways to care for piriformis syndrome are to take pain killers and work on strengthening the body. This often includes going to a physical therapist first and finding the best stretches for your body. Stretching the piriformis muscle often allows it to relieve tension, so your glutes are more comfortable.

Unlike the treatments before, it is best to use heat compressions to relax your muscles. Place the heat pad where you feel the most pain and wait for the heat to work its magic. Stretching helps the muscles to warm-up, but keeping heat on the wound for around half an hour will help it heal.

In extreme cases, the pain becomes so intense that these other treatments are not possible. Only for this case would you consider surgery. Removing part of the piriformis muscle would allow some tension release. However, as this is highly invasive, stick to the other treatments unless absolutely necessary.

Achilles Tendonitis

Achilles tendonitis refers to the pain felt from the ankle to the calf when experiencing high-impact sports. The ankle receives a lot of pressure when running because it is usually the first section of the leg to receive the brunt of the strike. The Achilles tendon connects the heel to the back of the calf, so any injury to the tendon can cause excessive pain in both areas.

Running, jumping, walking, or any other repetitious, hard-impact activities can cause Achilles tendonitis. The tendon becomes inflamed due to the pressure under which it is placed. It is also sometimes caused by poor technique or by events where you are running down hill, where the majority of your weight is concentrated on your flexed tendon.

It is most common to see swelling at the ankle after a run. It often becomes inflamed, causing the skin around it to stretch and burn. It may also become difficult to stretch your ankle when you stand. The tendon wishes to remain relaxed, so any contraction or extension can cause pain.

Prevention

Much of the prevention associated with Achilles tendonitis also applies to runner's knee. When running, take shorter steps to prevent your body from putting too much pressure on your ankle. If you are new to running, move slowly at first and gain speed and distance gradually, though that advice is sound for runners of any experience.

Take care of your feet. If you are wearing shoes that do not support your heels and ankles, you will likely see an emergence. Also, be smart about where you choose to run. Over flexing your ankle as you run can cause it to feel excess pressure. Running downhill or over rocky terrain are other common factors to Achilles tendonitis.

Treatment

As always, one of the best ways to treat Achilles tendonitis is to adjust the temperature at the source. Since the area is inflamed, apply pressure and a cold compress to reduce swelling. Try gently flexing your ankle to get the tendon moving while you ice it. When you can, try elevating the foot, allowing even blood flow and to prevent blood pooling in one spot.

Wear protective gear. If you have a boot or ankle support, use this while running. Though it may not completely solve your problem, it will highly benefit your situation and help you adjust to running once you have taken time off for stress. Achilles tendonitis is also commonly aggravated, so ease into whatever running technique you have after this injury.

Chapter 9: Step-By-Step Programs

Now that you have learned everything you need to know about running, it is time to put that knowledge into practice. This chapter contains eight programs to help you get started on your running journey. Whether you have been running for a long time or this is the first time you will be putting on running shoes, there is a program for you in this chapter.

Each program gives you advice for the week, so use it as a reference and come back to this chapter often. If you are struggling with an injury or do not know how to maintain some of these rigorous schedules, modify them or go back through the book and adjust your nutrition, warm-ups, cool downs, and basic techniques to keep you out on the road. Good luck!

30-Minute Running Programs

If you are just starting to run, you may feel overwhelmed with how fast many step-by-step programs are. However, if you are looking for a program to get you started, I have compiled some of the best to choose from. It takes time and patience to build up and be able to run long distances or for a long time, which is why it is important to listen to your body. The programs we cover now will give you the boost you need to run up to 30 minutes.

30 Days to 30-Minutes of Running

For those who are interested in an accelerated course, use this 30 Days to 30-Minutes of Running. There is no distance requirement, so running is based solely on endurance. During week one, begin to develop what you believe to be the perfect running routine. Though this program covers every other day from Monday to Friday, you can pick which days work for you and which will help you develop a stronger connection with running.

Before each run, develop your stretching routine. If you are new to running, plan for at least five minutes of stretching to give your muscles time to adjust to the new strain put on them. After each workout, stretch every muscle. Believe me, there will be some muscles that you did not know you had that will be sore the next morning.

Week 1
"The miracle isn't that I finished. The miracle is that I had the courage to start." *John Bingham*

Day 1 (10 minutes)	Run 1 minute Walk 1 minute *Repeat 4 times*
Day 3 (12 minutes)	Run 1 minute Walk 1 minute *Repeat 5 times*
Day 5 (14 minutes)	Run 1 minute Walk 1 minute *Repeat 6 times*

Week two steps it up to more difficult training. Instead of adding minutes to this run, you will also change your routine. If you find yourself out of breath after the first few minutes, slow your pace. If you find that the change of rhythm is too easy, increase your pace.

Week two is also the week of independence. Though the schedule listed below shows three days of running, try running on your own on off days. You do not have to follow the schedule listed below. Test your limits and get into the rhythm of running.

Week 2	
"Run when you can, walk if you have to, crawl if you must; just never give up." *Dean Karnazes*	
Day 8 (10 minutes)	Run 2 minutes Walk 1 minute Run 1 minute Walk 1 minute *Repeat once*
Day 10 (14 minutes)	Run 3 minutes Walk 1 minute Run 2 minute Walk 1 minute *Repeat once*
Day 12 (20 minutes)	Run 3 minutes Walk 1 minute *Repeat 4 times*

Week three is the middle of your program. At this point, you should feel your muscles become getting used to the strain of running. However, pay attention to what it is telling you and if you feel your body start to complain, relax the schedule and attend to your body's needs. Follow the steps for injury prevention and treatment.

By the end of week three, you should be running on your off days. "Free running" indicates your own schedule. Repeat the previous day's workout, or consider your own schedule. If you feel as though you can run for ten minutes with no walking breaks, test that theory. Develop a relationship with your body that lets you know when to push yourself and when to quit.

Week 3	
"I don't run to add days to my life, I run to add life to my days." *Ronald Rook*	
Day 15 (Run 20 minutes)	Run 5 minutes Walk 1 minute Run 3 minutes Walk 1 minute *Repeat once*
Day 16	Free running
Day 17 (28 minutes)	Run 6 minutes Walk 1 minute *Repeat 3 times*
Day 18	Free running
Day 19 (27 minutes)	Run 8 minutes Walk 1 minute *Repeat 2 times*
Day 20	Free running

As the last full week of running, it is time to develop your interest into a love for the sport. Find outside motivators to get you the rest of the way through the week. Running should be part of your daily routine. Find reasons to love running, and enjoy each improvement you have made over the course of the last three weeks.

This is the time of the running program that it becomes more and more difficult to continue running. Do not let that stop you! Review why you wanted to run and ask others to keep you honest. You can do this.

Week 4	
"The point is whether or not I improved over yesterday. In long-distance running the only opponent you have to beat is yourself, the way you used to be." *- Haruki Murakami*	
Day 21 (33 minutes)	Run 10 minutes Walk 1 minute *Repeat 2 times*
Day 22	Free running
Day 23 (32 minutes)	Run 15 minutes Walk 1 minute *Repeat once*
Day 24	Free running
Day 25 (32 minutes)	Run 20 minutes Walk 1 minute Run 10 minutes Walk 1 minute
Day 26	Free running

Once you have gotten to the final week of running, your body has likely become accustomed to the process of running. Congratulations! The final leg of the running program is to use the knowledge you have learned from listening to your body and magnify the best qualities.

Running should become somewhat of a ritual to you now. Use your free running days to care for injuries or incorporate your own schedule. If you feel ready to run 30 minutes before the end of the week, do it! The only way to develop a love for running is to run as often as you can.

Week 5	
"Every morning in Africa, a gazelle wakes up, it knows it must outrun the fastest lion or it will be killed. Every morning in Africa, a lion wakes up. It knows it must run faster than the slowest gazelle, or it will starve. It doesn't matter whether you're the lion or a gazelle – when the sun comes up, you'd better be running." -Christopher McDougall	
Day 29 (25 minutes)	Run 25 minutes *No walking*
Day 30	Free running
Day 31 (30 minutes)	Run 30 minutes *No walking*

45 Days to 30 Minutes of Running

Many people believe that the 30-day method is too labor intensive, and if you are just getting started, it is often good to consider slowing it down. The 45-day plan offers you just that. You will still see yourself running after 30 minutes, but you will see a significant decrease in joint trauma when you take the longer approach. If you suffer from joint injuries, take further pressure off by running on a treadmill or elliptical machine.

During week one, you are just warming up to running. Therefore, the first week is moderately easy. If you feel as though it is too easy, consider changing your pace. However, listen to your body. If you feel up to it, use your off-days to go for walks and increase your pace as you increase your time.

Week 1	
"I'll be happy if running and I can grow old together." *-Haruki Murakami*	
Day 1 (10 minutes)	Run 1 minute Walk 1 minute *Repeat 4 times*
Day 3 (12 minutes)	Run 1 minute Walk 1 minute *Repeat 5 times*
Day 5 (14 minutes)	Run 1 minute Walk 1 minute *Repeat 6 times*

When you enter week two, consider using the off-days to build up stamina. This means that you should work at a speed that is comfortable for your body, but work toward higher speeds and spend more time out on the road. If you only walk for 20 minutes, that is a step in the right direction. Do what feels natural and is helpful for your body.

Your second week focuses primarily on building your comfort with running. Instead of thinking that you have to make it some distance before you can slow down, become comfortable with the mindset that you do not have to satisfy a certain pace, only a certain time limit. If you find that a light jog suits your body the best right now, use that method. You are not constrained to work faster than you feel comfortable.

Week 2	
"Running is about finding your inner peace, and so is a life well lived." *-Dean Karnazes*	
Day 8 (15 minutes)	Run 2 minutes Walk 1 minute Run 1 minute Walk 1 minute *Repeat 2 times*
Day 10 (15 minutes)	Run 2 minutes Walk 1 minute *Repeat 4 times*
Day 12 (14 minutes)	Run 3 minutes Walk 1 minute Run 2 minutes Walk 1 minute *Repeat once*

Week three is the beginning of your independence from the schedule. The free runs listed here could refer to brisk walks or testing your limits. Either option will get your body more accustomed to moving every day. Use these days as an opportunity to grow your connection with running.

Begin to think about how to best take care of your body. If you feel pain anywhere, take the time to address it instead of simply ignoring it and moving on. Always practice preventative care to avoid injuries, and develop a strong dependence on warm-up and post-workout stretches.

Week 3	

"Running isn't a sport for pretty boys… It's about the sweat in your hair and the blisters on your feet. It's the frozen spit on your chin and the nausea in your gut. It's about throbbing calves and cramps at midnight that are strong enough to wake the dead. It's about getting out the door and running when the rest of the world is only dreaming about having the passion that you need to live each and every day with. It's about being on a lonely road and running like a champion even when there's not a single soul in sight to cheer you on. Running is all about having the desire to train and persevere until every fiber in your legs, mind, and heart is turned to steel. And when you've finally forged hard enough, you will have become the best runner you can be. And that's all that you can ask for."
-Paul Maurer

Day 15 (16 minutes)	Run 3 minutes Walk 1 minute *Repeat 3 times*
Day 16	Free running
Day 17 (16 minutes)	Run 4 minutes Walk 1 minute Run 2 minutes Walk 1 minute *Repeat once*
Day 18	Free running
Day 19 (20 minutes)	Run 4 minutes Walk 1 minute *Repeat 3 times*
Day 20	Free running

Week four marks the halfway mark in your journey. Congratulations! Most habits are created after consistently practicing them for three weeks. Week four should also indicate that your joints are becoming accustomed to the motion and pressure given every day.

Though the first few weeks are often difficult, you may start feeling the passion and regular thoughts of running during week four. As soon as you hit this stage, it is easier to continue running for the love of exercise and how you feel while active. Become accustomed to running every day. On your free run days, focus on your ability to continue a jogging pace. Since you have already run for three weeks, your free running workouts should include longer periods of running than walking.

Week 4	
"Running! If there's any activity happier, more exhilarating, more nourishing to the imagination, I can't think of what it might be. In running the mind flees with the body, the mysterious efflorescence of language seems to pulse in the brain, in rhythm with our feet and the swinging of our arms." *-Joyce Carol Oats*	
Day 22 (20 minutes)	Run 5 minutes Walk 1 minute Run 3 minutes Walk 1 minute *Repeat once*
Day 23	Free running
Day 24 (24 minutes)	Run 5 minutes Walk 1 minute *Repeat 3 times*
Day 25	Free running

Week 4	
Day 26 (26 minutes)	Run 7 minutes Walk 1 minute Run 4 minutes Walk 1 minute *Repeat once*
Day 27	Free running

Week five builds your endurance. Instead of alternating running patterns, the week sticks to one formula: run for several minutes and walk for one. Experiment with pace. Though it may seem simple to walk when you feel tired, instead keep your motion constant but change the pace. If you are having difficulties maintaining pace, ask a friend to join you. It is easier to work in a group than it is alone.

On your free days, experiment with your endurance. Run for your whole session if you can, even if that means that you are moving at one mile per hour. Begin to connect with your body to feel which muscles are working where. If you feel pain, adjust your running technique to better suit your running style.

Week 5	
"Crossing the starting line may be an act of courage, but crossing the finish line is an act of faith. Faith is what keeps us going when nothing else will. Faith is the emotion that will give you victory over your past, the demons in your soul, and all of those voices that tell you what you can and cannot do and can and cannot be." *-John Bingham*	
Day 29 (27 minutes)	Run 8 minutes Walk 1 minute *Repeat 2 times*
Day 30	Free running
Day 31 (33 minutes)	Run 10 minutes Walk 1 minute *Repeat 2 times*
Day 32	Free running
Day 33 (39 minutes)	Run 12 minutes Walk 1 minute *Repeat 2 times*
Day 34	Free running

Week six is the final full week of training. Take advantage of the time to build your stamina. Test and push yourself to your limits. Use the free run days to either recover or push your previous records. Improve your running technique and treat endurance injuries as soon as possible.

Week 6	
"I run because if I didn't, I'd be sluggish and glum and spend too much time on the couch. I run to breathe the fresh air. I run to explore. I run to escape the ordinary. I run...to savor the trip along the way. Life becomes a little more vibrant, a little more intense. I like that." *-Dean Karnazes*	
Day 36 (32 minutes)	Run 15 minutes Walk 1 minute *Repeat once*
Day 37	Free running
Day 38 (32 minutes)	Run 20 minutes Walk 1 minute Run 10 minutes Walk 1 minute
Day 39	Free running
Day 40 (25 minutes)	Run 25 minutes
Day 41	Free running

You have reached the final week. Congratulations! It is difficult to maintain a schedule when the going gets tough. However, because you made it to this point, you are only a few days away from achieving your goal of running for 30 minutes.

Now that you have completed much of the program, make running your own. Develop a soundtrack to encourage yourself to run. Set goals to improve your performance in the next few weeks. The hardest part of starting a goal is maintaining the motivation to see it through. Because of your persistence, you have made your dreams come true.

Week 7
"The Hopis consider running a form of prayer; they offer every step as a sacrifice to a loved one, and in return ask the Great Spirit to match their strength with some of his own."   *-Christopher McDougall*

Day 43 (27 minutes)	Run 27 minutes
Day 44	Free running
Day 45 (30 minutes)	Run 30 minutes

60-Minute Running Program

Running for long periods of time can be rewarding, but it is often difficult to find the best way to achieve these goals, especially if you are just starting. These 60-minute running programs are designed to help you achieve your goal for running for long periods of time in short time frames.

Before you begin, develop stretching techniques that help you best. Follow the nutritional guides to help your body sustain your running goals. You will notice in these programs that the accelerated rate requires you to run consistently with the programs set in place and to put in your own time to push boundaries and allow for recovery time. These courses are intended for people who consistently exercise and are up to the rigorous routine.

30 Days to 60 Minutes of Running

Week one is the beginning of a rigorous fast track to running for an hour. You will notice that each day requires you to run a minute longer than before. It is vital in this program that you follow correct injury prevention techniques since you are subjecting your body to an accelerated pace.

Since you have chosen this running routine, it is time to get cracking on proper techniques. Ask a friend to join you to encourage you to get out of bed every morning and prepare for the run ahead.

Week 1	
"Some seek the comfort of their therapist's office, other head to the corner pub and dive into a pint, but I chose running as my therapy." *-Dean Karnazes*	
Day 1 (20 minutes)	Run 1 minute Walk 1 minute *Repeat 9 times*
Day 3 (21 minutes)	Run 2 minutes Walk 1 minute *Repeat 6 times*
Day 5 (24 minutes)	Run 3 minutes Walk 1 minute *Repeat 5 times*

Week two has begun and it is time to head out to the pavement. You will probably feel sore, so drink a lot of water. Stretch out those muscles and prepare them for this week's rigorous course. Last week gradually led up to running for three minutes and walking for one. You will notice that this week is more intense. That means that you need to focus on eating enough food to sustain your workouts.

Start to consider running on your days off. Week three introduces free running days, which allow you to test your limits, so it is best to work up to that now. Do not train so intensely that you feel pain, but see how far you can run without stopping. Even if you slow down to a mile an hour, keep running.

Week 2	
"Pain is inevitable. Suffering is optional." -Haruki Murakami	
Day 8 (30 minutes)	Run 5 minutes Walk 1 minute *Repeat 4 times*
Day 10 (32 minutes)	Run 7 minutes Walk 1 minute *Repeat 3 times*
Day 12 (33 minutes)	Run 10 minutes Walk 1 minute *Repeat 2 times*

Week three brings the free running days. If you are new to running, you can use these days to walk, or you can practice running as long as you can without stopping. Running times for every other day improve dramatically as you learn how to maintain a running pace for long periods of time.

When many hit the midway point, it is common to want to give up. After all, your accelerated course feels difficult to maintain. Do not let this stop you. Write down the reasons for running in the first place. Whether you want to become an athlete or help your mental health, there is always a reason to continue. Have friends and family hold you accountable for your progress and push forward.

Week 3

"People sometimes sneer at those who run every day, claiming they'll go to any length to live longer. But don't think that's the reason most people run. Most runners run not because they want to live longer, but because they want to live life to the fullest. If you're going to while away the years, it's far better to live them with clear goals and fully alive then in a fog, and I believe running helps you to do that. Exerting yourself to the fullest within your individual limits: that's the essence of running, and a metaphor for life – and for me, for writing as whole. I believe many runners would agree."
-Haruki Murakami

Day 15 (39 minutes)	Run 12 minutes Walk 1 minute *Repeat 2 times*
Day 16	Free running
Day 17 (48 minutes)	Run 15 minutes Walk 1 minute *Repeat 2 times*
Day 18	Free running
Day 19 (57 minutes)	Run 18 minutes Walk 1 minute *Repeat 2 times*
Day 20	Free running

The final full week of running has arrived, meaning that the training program will increase dramatically. You are responsible for consistently running, and free running days should be used to enhance your stamina. Remember, if you are feeling aches and pains, take them seriously. Since this week is accelerated, take special care of your body. Identify any problem areas and treat them immediately. If you feel faint during runs, return to Chapter 2 to review correct nutrition.

Though free running days are determined by you, notice that the scheduled days increase by ten minutes every other day. Use those free days to slowly build up to longer runs. Consider adding another five minutes to every run on your free running days.

Week 4	
"Struggling and suffering are the essence of a life worth living. If you're not pushing yourself beyond the comfort zone, if you're not demanding more from yourself – expanding and learning as you go – you're choosing a numb existence. You're denying yourself an extraordinary trip." *-Dean Karnazes*	
Day 22 (52 minutes)	Run 25 minutes Walk 1 minute *Repeat once*
Day 23	Free running
Day 24 (72 minutes)	Run 35 minutes Walk 1 minute *Repeat once*
Day 25	Free running
Day 26 (46 minutes)	Run 45 minutes Walk 1 minute
Day 27	Free running

You have reached the final week of your running routine. Congratulations! That means that you have fought through the difficult month and succeeded. This week, you will run for 60 minutes. You are adding an additional 15 minutes to your last run, so listen to your body and enjoy the experience. You have earned it.

Week 5	
"If you don't have answers to your problems after a four-hour run, you ain't getting them." -*Christopher McDougall*	
Day 29 (60 minutes)	Run 60 minutes
Day 30	Free running

45 Days to 60 Minutes of Running

If you want to work toward 60 minutes of running but do not want to take such an accelerated course, choose 45 days to 60 minutes of running. This is still a highly intensive program, so be prepared to work quickly.

Week one is important because it gets your feet under you in the running world. You may be incredibly fit or this may be your first day putting on your running shoes, but this program is possible for anyone who has enough motivation to continue. Build up to 30 minutes of running by slowly adding minutes to your running regime. If you are struggling to keep up with the schedule, slow your pace as you run.

Drink as much water as you can in your first week to prepare for future weeks. Your muscles will be sore after running at an accelerated pace for the first time, so take supplements that will help your body recover quickly.

Week 1	
"Pain is temporary. Quitting lasts forever." *-Lance Armstrong*	
Day 1 (20 minutes)	Run 1 minute Walk 1 minute *Repeat 9 times*
Day 3 (24 minutes)	Run 3 minutes Walk 1 minute *Repeat 5 times*
Day 5 (30 minutes)	Run 5 minutes Walk 1 minute *Repeat 4 times*

Reaching week two means that you have successfully run 30 minutes and you are ready to up your game. Consider adding free running days to your schedule, which will help you build up stamina for days to come. Find the motivation to keep running for those long minutes. Even if your pace slows to a crawl, keep moving forward. You are working toward 60 minutes of running, not a specific distance.

Listen to your body as you complete this week. If you experience injuries, take time off to recover. Though it may seem tough to soldier on through your pain, it is detrimental to your running career in the long run.

Week 2	
"Your body will argue that there is no justifiable reason to continue. Your only recourse is to call on your spirit, which fortunately functions independently of logic." *-Tim Noakes*	
Day 8 (32 minutes)	Run 7 minutes Walk 1 minute *Repeat 3 times*
Day 10 (30 minutes)	Run 9 minutes Walk 1 minute *Repeat 2 times*
Day 12 (36 minutes)	Run 11 minutes Walk 1 minute *Repeat 2 times*

Week three is the beginning of the free running days. These are essential to keep you running throughout the week. If you want to achieve your 60-minutes in 45 days goal, you must use these days to improve your body. Whether that means taking a day to only walk or to push yourself to run longer than you have before, your body will appreciate the attention.

Your body may also start to feel the strain of running consistently, especially if you do not exercise regularly. Keep following your goal, but remember that your body is the boss of the road. If you can continue running for long periods of time, do so. If you feel yourself starting to slip, slip constructively. Keep your mind focused on your goal and keep your body comfortable at the same time.

Week 3	
"All I do is keep on running in my own cozy, homemade void, my own nostalgic silence. And this is a pretty wonderful thing. No matter what anybody else says." *-Haruki Murakami*	
Day 15 (42 minutes)	Run 13 minutes Walk 1 minute *Repeat 2 times*
Day 16	Free running
Day 17 (48 minutes)	Run 15 minutes Walk 1 minute *Repeat 2 times*
Day 18	Free running
Day 19 (54 minutes)	Run 17 minutes Walk 1 minute *Repeat 2 times*
Day 20	Free running

Week four marks the middle of your running routine. Habits are often built after 21 days, so you have made it past some of the most crucial periods. The mind can be a terrible place, especially if it constantly tells you to quit. Do not let your mind destroy your progress. Strive for success and aim for working more consistently.

Week 4	
"People think I'm crazy to put myself through such torture, though I would argue otherwise. Somewhere along the line, we seem to have confused comfort with happiness. Dostoyevsky had it right: 'Suffering is the sole origin of consciousness.' Never are my senses more engaged than when the pain sets in. There is a magic in misery. Just ask any runner." *-Dean Karnazes*	
Day 22 (42 minutes)	Run 20 minutes Walk 1 minute *Repeat once*
Day 23	Free running
Day 24 (46 minutes)	Run 22 minutes Walk 1 minute *Repeat once*
Day 25	Free running
Day 26 (50 minutes)	Run 24 minutes Walk 1 minute *Repeat once*
Day 27	Free running

Week five is the last week with the same schedule of adding two minutes to every run. This time frame is excellent for testing your supplements and locking in your nutritional schedule. If you feel you are becoming more tired from the strenuous schedule, take a good look at your supplement intake and adjust them to give yourself more energy.

At this point, you may feel excess strain on your legs and feet. Running is a high-impact sport, so it is normal to feel this way, but this is no excuse to slow down on your warm-ups.

Instead, your pre-workout and post-workout stretches should become an integral part of your runs.

Week 5	
"There is something magical about running; after a certain distance, it transcends the body. Then a bit further, it transcends the mind. A bit further yet, and what you have before you, laid bare, is the soul." *-Kristin Armstrong*	
Day 29 (54 minutes)	Run 26 minutes Walk 1 minute *Repeat once*
Day 30	Free running
Day 31 (58 minutes)	Run 28 minutes Walk 1 minute *Repeat once*
Day 32	Free running
Day 33 (62 minutes)	Run 30 minutes Walk 1 minute *Repeat once*
Day 34	Free running

Week six is the final full week of your training, and this includes hitting the track more often. Instead of the usual two minute increases every other day, the schedule increases exponentially to an additional five minutes. On your free running days, take care of your body, rest, walk, or continue to run. Keep in mind that the increased strain may cause discomfort or pain. If you take a day off, it will not substantially affect your performance the next day.

The last two days of the weed include running, but do not let this deter you. The week was structured to give you less time on the track to make up for the loss in overall time.

Week 6	
"If you are losing faith in human nature, go out and watch a marathon." *-Katherine Switzer*	
Day 36 (72 minutes)	Run 35 minutes Walk 1 minute *Repeat once*
Day 37	Free running
Day 38 (41 minutes)	Run 40 minutes Walk 1 minute
Day 39	Free running
Day 40 (46 minutes)	Run 45 minutes Walk 1 minute
Day 41 (51 minutes)	Run 50 minutes Walk 1 minute

Week seven is the final week in the program. Congratulations! You have made it to the end. This is a short week that also provides a free running day to allow you to recuperate or push your boundaries right before your final run. Good luck!

Week 7	
"There is nothing so momentary as a sporting achievement, and nothing so lasting as the memory of it." *-Greg Dening*	
Day 43 (56 minutes)	Run 55 minutes Walk 1 minute
Day 44	Free running
Day 45 (60 minutes)	Run 60 minutes *No walking*

Weight-Loss Running Program

Weight loss is one of the primary reasons most people choose to run. Running paired with other cardio activities give your body the necessary stress to work many different muscles throughout the week. Because running is a full-body exercise, working other parts of the body is essential to creating a form that can last through endurance running.

There is no distance limit for these exercises, so develop your cardio at your discretion. Though you are working toward weight loss, continue to work toward long-distance running, which will ultimately burn more calories than short-distance running. You burn 100 calories for every mile you complete—walking or running—so find motivation to continue gaining distance by working with friends and family.

Running for 4 Weeks of Weight Loss

Week one gives you your first look at the various kinds of cardio to do on your off days. Remember that building strong muscles will aid you in any type of running, so if you wish to work on body-weight exercises, you will still see results throughout this weight loss journey.

Running can be boring if you do not have anyone to run with or you do not have a proper music mix. Break up the boredom by running both forward and backward. You will use different muscles, and the new routine will give you a break from the high-impact motion.

Week 1	
"Running is real and relatively simple... but it ain't easy." *-Mark Will-Weber*	
Day 1 (10 minutes)	Run 1 minute Walk 1 minute *Repeat 4 times*
Day 2 (20 minutes)	Perform low-impact cardio such as swimming, walking, or biking
Day 3 (15 minutes)	Run 2 minutes Walk 1 minute *Repeat 4 times*
Day 4	Rest
Day 5 (15 minutes)	Run 2 minutes Walk 1 minute *Repeat 4 times*
Day 6 (20 minutes)	Perform low-impact cardio such as swimming, walking, or biking
Day 7 (20 minutes)	Run 3 minutes Walk 1 minute *Repeat 4 times*

During week two, change up your routine by choosing low-impact cardio different from week one. Explore your warm-ups and enjoy stretching before and after every exercise. If you feel your joints start to ache when hitting the pavement, try an elliptical to give your joints a break while still getting the cardio you need.

This week, focus on the way you move your body. Proper posture guarantees a more comfortable run. You may also be surprised which muscles become sore after working out muscles that are not usually stretched. Drink a lot of water to keep your body hydrated and to prevent soreness. Ù

Week 2	
"How to run an ultramarathon? Puff out your chest, put one foot in front of the other, and don't stop til you cross the finish line." *-Dean Karnazes*	
Day 8 (20 minutes)	Run 3 minutes Walk 1 minute *Repeat 4 times*
Day 9 (20 minutes)	Perform low-impact cardio such as yoga, rowing, or climbing stairs
Day 10 (25 minutes)	Run 4 minutes Walk 1 minute *Repeat 4 times*
Day 11	Rest
Day 12 (25 minutes)	Run 4 minutes Walk 1 minute *Repeat 4 times*
Day 13 (20 minutes)	Perform low-impact cardio such as yoga, rowing, or climbing stairs
Day 14 (30 minutes)	Run 5 minutes Walk 1 minute *Repeat 4 times*

The beginning of week three signals the middle of the program. Use this opportunity to examine how your running can improve. If you feel pain in your joints, stretch more before and after the workout and examine your diet. Remember the supplements suggested are not quick fixes, but they do help over time. Trust your body and adjust your exercise to accommodate the way you feel.

This week focus on endurance. How long can you go before you start to feel like you have pushed your boundaries? If you need to, slow your pace enough that you can take a breather while still running. Use the off days to practice a new type of cardio. Even if you do not have extra equipment, you can still use nature to give you a low-impact exercise.

Week 3	
"Ask nothing from your running, in other words, and you'll get more than you ever imagined." *-Chris McDougall*	
Day 15 (30 minutes)	Run 5 minutes Walk 1 minute *Repeat 4 times*
Day 16 (30 minutes)	Perform low-impact cardio such as boxing, jump rope, or Zumba
Day 17 (35 minutes)	Run 6 minutes Walk 1 minute *Repeat 4 times*
Day 18	Rest
Day 19 (35 minutes)	Run 6 minutes Walk 1 minute *Repeat 4 times*

Week 3	
Day 20 (30 minutes)	Perform low-impact cardio such as boxing, jump rope, or Zumba
Day 21 (40 minutes)	Run 7 minutes Walk 1 minute *Repeat 4 times*

Week four is the final week in the 4 weeks to weight loss program. As such, take advantage of the time you have to explore how to incorporate running into your weekly routine after the course is finished. Once you start running consistently, do not stop.

This week focus on making running more enjoyable for yourself. Try a new playlist or sign up for a local running club. If you do not want to spend the money on an expensive gym membership, encourage friends and family to exercise with you. Encouraging each other even across long distances will keep you accountable for keeping up with your running.

Week 4	
"It was being a runner that mattered, not how fast or how far I could run. The joy was in the act of running and in the journey, not in the destination." *-John Bingham*	
Day 22 (40 minutes)	Run 7 minutes Walk 1 minute *Repeat 4 times*
Day 23 (30 minutes)	Perform low-impact cardio such as walking, calisthenics, or yoga

Week 4	
Day 24 (45 minutes)	Run 8 minutes Walk 1 minute *Repeat 4 times*
Day 25	Rest
Day 26 (45 minutes)	Run 8 minutes Walk 1 minute *Repeat 4 times*
Day 27 (30 minutes)	Perform low-impact cardio such as walking, calisthenics, or yoga
Day 28 (50 minutes)	Run 9 minutes Walk 1 minute *Repeat 4 times*

Running for 8 Weeks of Weight Loss

If you want a more intense workout over the course of 8 weeks, choose the running for 8 weeks of weight loss program. You will experience much of the same exercises from the 4 week program, but this training program is more specific. The running exercises allow for gradual improvement over time. You are not required to run at a specific pace or distance, so use the timing at your discretion.

Week one is about starting your journey into a weight-loss journey. Get your feet under you by performing warm-ups before and post-workout stretches after exercising. Part of the goal of this week is to help you get used to working out nearly every day. On the off days, you will perform low-impact cardio to get your heart rate up, but it will not be so hard on your joints, especially if you are new to running.

This week, focus on becoming comfortable with your posture as you run. Instead of leaning forward, try to rock back on your heels slightly to take the pressure off the balls of your feet. Once you get the hang of running, put on more speed and experiment with how your posture affects you.

Week 1	
"Getting more exercise isn't only good for your waistline. It's a natural antidepressant, that leaves you in a great mood." *-Auliq Ice*	
Day 1 (10 minutes)	Run 1 minute Walk 1 minute *Repeat 4 times*
Day 2 (20 minutes)	Perform low-impact cardio: Walking
Day 3 (15 minutes)	Run 2 minutes Walk 1 minute *Repeat 4 times*
Day 4	Rest
Day 5 (15 minutes)	Run 2 minutes Walk 1 minute *Repeat 4 times*
Day 6 (20 minutes)	Perform low-impact cardio: Biking

Week 1	
Day 7 (20 minutes)	Run 3 minutes Walk 1 minute *Repeat 4 times*

Week two is about making your body stronger. You may feel the strain in your feet and legs as you work up to consistently working out. If you are not used to exercising so frequently, slow down, but do not stop. If you need to go slower in running or calisthenics, do so. Listen to your body and develop ways to improve your mindset about exercising.

If your body experiences pain, examine it immediately. Though it is common to believe that pain means that you are improving, you should only exercise until you are uncomfortable. Pain means there is something wrong with the body. It is better to take care of yourself now than subjecting yourself to days, weeks, or months of painful recovery.

Week 2	
"Try jogging when following your heart, it's healthier." *-Benny Bellamacina*	
Day 8 (20 minutes)	Run 3 minutes Walk 1 minute *Repeat 4 times*

Week 2	
Day 9 (20 minutes)	Perform low-impact cardio: Calisthenics 1 minute squats 1 minute high plank 1 minute front lunges 1 minute crunches 1 minute burpees *Repeat 3 times*
Day 10 (25 minutes)	Run 4 minutes Walk 1 minute *Repeat 4 times*
Day 11	Rest
Day 12 (25 minutes)	Run 4 minutes Walk 1 minute *Repeat 4 times*
Day 13 (20 minutes)	Perform low-impact cardio: Rowing
Day 14 (30 minutes)	Run 5 minutes Walk 1 minute *Repeat 4 times*

Week three is about finding a balance. You should have your nutrition nailed down, or at least working toward doing so. Find the balance between exercise and diet that will help you lose weight the fastest. Remember that you must have a deficit of at least 500 calories in your normal caloric budget to lose weight. For every calorie you burn, add half its value to your caloric budget.

Week 3	
"What I've learned from running is that the time to push hard is when you're hurting like crazy and you want to give up. Success is often just around the corner." *-James Dyson*	
Day 15 (30 minutes)	Run 5 minutes Walk 1 minute *Repeat 4 times*
Day 16 (25 minutes)	Perform low-impact cardio: Hiking
Day 17 (35 minutes)	Run 6 minutes Walk 1 minute *Repeat 4 times*
Day 18	Rest
Day 19 (35 minutes)	Run 6 minutes Walk 1 minute *Repeat 4 times*
Day 20 (25 minutes)	Perform low-impact cardio: Biking
Day 21 (40 minutes)	Run 7 minutes Walk 1 minute *Repeat 4 times*

Week four is about setting up the motivation to continue to work toward your goal, especially when the going gets tough. It is normal to feel as though a tough training program is too much work. In fact, that is why most people quit. They work hard for the first few weeks then fall into a rut, claiming that they deserve to take a week off. Do not fall into this trap. Keep striving for your goal and make yourself accountable for your exercising by utilizing apps, friends, or family. By the end of this week, you are halfway through the program, so keep it up.

Week 4	
"I'm often asked what I think about as I run. Usually, the people who ask this have never run long distances themselves. I always ponder the question. What exactly do I think about when I'm running? I don't have a clue." *-Haruki Murakami*	
Day 22 (40 minutes)	Run 7 minutes Walk 1 minute *Repeat 4 times*
Day 23 (25 minutes)	Perform low-impact cardio: Calisthenics 1 minute push ups 1 minute side lunges 1 minute elbow planks 1 minute jumping jacks 1 minute burpees *Repeat 4 times*
Day 24 (45 minutes)	Run 8 minutes Walk 1 minute *Repeat 4 times*
Day 25	Rest
Day 26 (45 minutes)	Run 8 minutes Walk 1 minute *Repeat 4 times*

Week 4	
Day 27 (25 minutes)	Perform low-impact cardio: Walking
Day 28 (50 minutes)	Run 9 minutes Walk 1 minute *Repeat 4 times*

As the minutes to run slowly climb every day, be sure to keep track of how your body is coping. Take a moment to review how your body has improved and what you can still do to complete the training. If you feel worn out, adjust your supplements and make sure you are getting enough rest, both of which play significant roles in determining the efficiency of a run.

Week five is about accountability. Start a journal about your eating and running habits. Record any other activity that you do throughout the day. As you see your weight start to decrease, keep track of your progress. If you have not already done so, start weighing yourself regularly. Develop a way to track your progress to maintain your motivation.

Week 5	
"But you can't muscle through a five-hour run that way; you have to relax into it like easing your body into a hot bath, until it no longer resists the shock and begins to enjoy it." *-Christopher McDougall*	
Day 29 (50 minutes))	Run 9 minutes Walk 1 minute *Repeat 4 times*

Week 5	
Day 30 (30 minutes)	Perform low-impact cardio: Hiking
Day 31 (55 minutes)	Run 10 minutes Walk 1 minute *Repeat 4 times*
Day 32	Rest
Day 33 (55 minutes)	Run 10 minutes Walk 1 minute *Repeat 4 times*
Day 34 (30 minutes)	Perform low-impact cardio: Biking
Day 35 (60 minutes)	Run 11 minutes Walk 1 minute *Repeat 4 times*

Week six is about pushing yourself. You are more than halfway through the training, and it is time to push yourself to your boundaries. If you feel your pace is too slow on runs, increase it. If you feel you would benefit from variations of low-impact cardio, change it. Be aware of how your body is changing and push yourself.

Week 6	
"Adversity causes some men to break; others to break records." *-William Arthur Ward*	
Day 36 (60 minutes)	Run 11 minutes Walk 1 minute *Repeat 4 times*
Day 37 (30 minutes)	Perform low-impact cardio: Calisthenics 1 minute lunges 1 minute bicycle crunches 1 minute squats 1 minute standing crunches 1 minute burpees *Repeat 5 times*
Day 38 (65 minutes)	Run 12 minutes Walk 1 minute *Repeat 4 times*
Day 39	Rest
Day 40 (65 minutes)	Run 12 minutes Walk 1 minute *Repeat 4 times*
Day 41 (30 minutes)	Perform low-impact cardio: Walking
Day 42 (70 minutes)	Run 13 minutes Walk 1 minute *Repeat 4 times*

Week seven is about extending your workouts. As you can see from this week's schedule, you will run for over an hour, but use this opportunity to extend your workouts in other ways. If you have a desk job, perform sitting workouts throughout the day. If you have a highly intensive job that requires a lot of movement, up your game by throwing in additional squats, lunges, or twists.

Week 7	
"Every run is a work of art, a drawing on each day's canvas. Some runs are shouts and some runs are whispers. Some runs are eulogies and others celebrations." *-Dagny Scott Barrio*	
Day 43 (70 minutes)	Run 13 minutes Walk 1 minute *Repeat 4 times*
Day 44 (35 minutes)	Perform low-impact cardio: Jabs, hooks, and uppercuts
Day 45 (75 minutes)	Run 14 minutes Walk 1 minute *Repeat 4 times*
Day 46	Rest
Day 47 (75 minutes)	Run 14 minutes Walk 1 minute *Repeat 4 times*
Day 48 (35 minutes)	Perform low-impact cardio: Walking

Week 7	
Day 49 (80 minutes)	Run 15 minutes Walk 1 minute *Repeat 4 times*

Week eight, your final week, is about creating your own schedule to continue exercising after this training is complete. If you wish to go back and start over, do so. However, if you want to push yourself, create a different schedule that works best for you and push yourself to achieve it. The best way to achieve a goal is to set it.

During your final week, consider taking up additional forms of cardio exercise including martial arts, boxing, or weight lifting. All of these activities will help you work out in the future by building your lung capacity and endurance.

Week 8	
"I run because long after my footprints fade away, maybe I will have inspired a few to reject the easy path, hit the trails, put one foot in front of the other, and come to the same conclusion I did: I run because it always takes me where I want to go." *-Dean Karnazes*	
Day 50 (80 minutes)	Run 15 minutes Walk 1 minute *Repeat 4 times*

Week 8	
Day 51 (35 minutes)	Perform low-impact cardio: Calisthenics 1 minute low plank 1 minute jumping jacks 1 minute push ups 1 minute skier jumps 1 minute burpees *Repeat 6 times*
Day 52 (85 minutes)	Run 16 minutes Walk 1 minute *Repeat 4 times*
Day 53	Rest
Day 54 (85 minutes)	Run 16 minutes Walk 1 minute *Repeat 4 times*
Day 55 (35 minutes)	Perform low-impact cardio as Day 44
Day 56 (90 minutes))	Run 17 minutes Walk 1 minute *Repeat 4 times*

Running for Distance

"The journey of 1000 miles starts with a single step," or so the saying goes. Whether you are looking for a challenge after you have started your running journey or you just want to increase your speed over distance, these programs will guide you through your next adventure.

Increasing your running distance is incredibly rewarding, and it is the next step for many people who want to run races. Marathon runners have to start their own running regimens months or years in advance, before they take the plunge to last 26 miles. To become a long distance runner, the key is to start small and work your way up.

Unlike the previous running programs, the running for distance program utilizes miles instead of minutes to run. If you prefer using minutes instead, calculate the average time it takes you to run a mile and insert that number into the regimen instead. However, as you gain distance, the time it takes for you to complete a mile will change. Time yourself often to get an accurate estimate.

Build Up to 2 Miles

Running that first mile is a big step, but it is only the beginning. If you want to rack up the miles every week, you need to set a goal, and 2 miles is a great place to start. If you are training to run for long distances or just want to reach this goal, put your inhibitions behind and start to run.

This training program assumes that you are starting from square one, so week one gets you started to run. The free-running day is for you to either push yourself, rest or try some other cardio activity that will help you achieve your goal. Week one is about starting slowing and getting your bearings. Wear a pedometer or a sport watch to accurately gauge how many miles you have run, or a treadmill will do the calculations for you.

Week 1	
"If you don't think you were born to run you're not only denying history. You're denying who you are." *-Christopher McDougall*	
Day 1 (1 mile)	Run ¼ mile Walk ¼ mile *Repeat once*
Day 2	Rest
Day 3 (1 mile)	Run ¼ mile Walk ¼ mile *Repeat once*
Day 4	Free running
Day 5 (1 mile)	Run ½ mile Walk ¼ mile Run ¼ mile
Day 6	Rest
Day 7 (1 mile)	Run ½ mile Walk ¼ mile Run ¼ mile

Week two increases your distance by half a mile while maintaining the same distance to run. This is designed to increase your endurance. Instead of finishing after you have run once, you will learn to take a short break in between runs to become more productive. Push yourself at the final running stage by sprinting. You may run out of breath faster, but it will eventually improve your lung capacity over time.

Week 2	
"Jogging is very beneficial. It's good for your legs and your feet. It's also very good for the ground. It makes it feel needed." -*Charles M. Schulz*	
Day 8 (1 mile)	Run ¾ mile Walk ¼ mile
Day 9	Rest
Day 10 (1 mile)	Run ¾ mile Walk ¼ mile
Day 11	Free running
Day 12 (1 ½ miles)	Run ¾ mile Walk ½ mile Run ¼ mile
Day 13	Rest
Day 14 (1 ½ miles)	Run ¾ mile Walk ½ mile Run ¼ mile

The beginning of week three is the halfway point of the training program, so become accustomed to running most days of the week. Try running in intervals by sprinting for ¼ mile, jogging for ¼ mile, then repeating the process.

The only thing that will stop you from running further is your mind, so tell yourself that you can do it. The mind can be a negative agent in learning to run, telling you that your body cannot finish the run, but it can also be an instrument to help you push your body further than you thought it could go. Use your mind to your advantage.

Week 3	
"Yes, I am round. Yes, I am slow. Yes, I run as though my legs are tied together at the knees. But I am running. And that is all that matters." -*John Bingham*	
Day 15 (1 ½ miles)	Run 1 mile Walk ½ mile
Day 16	Rest
Day 17 (1 ½ miles)	Run 1 mile Walk ½ mile
Day 18	Free running
Day 19 (1 ½ miles)	Run 1 ¼ miles Walk ¼ mile
Day 20	Rest
Day 21 (1 ½ miles)	Run 1 ¼ mile Walk ¼ mile

In the final week of your training, develop a strong mental resolve to continue training after this program is complete. If you have not already tried one of the other programs, encourage yourself to try something new. If you are aiming to train for a marathon, either follow the pattern of this training or try calculating your running by minutes instead of miles. Whatever you do, do not give up running.

Week 4	
"Your body provides you with constant feedback that can help improve your running performance while minimizing biomechanical stress. Learn to differentiate between the discomfort of effort and the pain of injury. When you practice listening, you increase competence in persevering through the former and responding with respect and compassion to the latter." *-Gina Greenlee*	
Day 22 (2 miles)	Run 1 ½ miles Walk ½ mile
Day 23	Rest
Day 24 (2 miles)	Run 1 ½ miles Walk ½ mile
Day 25	Free running
Day 26 (2 miles)	Run 2 miles *No walking*
Day 27	Rest
Day 28 (2 miles)	Run 2 miles *No walking*

Build Up to 5 Miles

Five miles is a long distance, especially if you are just starting out. Do not let that deter you, however. Anything you set your mind to, you can achieve. The program is broken into five weeks, adding another mile every week. If you are uncomfortable with the fast pace, consider starting with one of the other programs and come back to this one later.

Week one is the week to get you out the door. You will be running for short distances, but they add up to a mile. On the free running day, consider running the full mile in preparation for the rest of the week. If you need a change of pace, choose another cardio workout such as swimming, biking, or walking to supplement the work you do on the track.

Week 1	
"After joyfully working each morning, I would leave off around midday to challenge myself to a footrace. Speeding along the sunny paths of the Jardin du Luxembourg, ideas would breed like aphids in my head – for creative invention is easy and sublime when air cycles quickly through the lungs and the body is busy at noble tasks." *-Roman Payne*	
Day 1 (1 mile)	Run ¼ mile Walk ¼ mile *Repeat once*
Day 2	Rest
Day 3 (1 mile)	Run ¼ mile Walk ¼ mile *Repeat once*
Day 4	Free running
Day 5 (1 mile)	Run ½ mile Walk ½ mile
Day 6	Rest
Day 7 (1 mile)	Run ½ mile Walk ½ mile

Week two should mark the beginning of your dependence on a pedometer or other device that will accurately mark how many steps you have taken. Most cell phones come with step counters built in, so you do not need to buy an additional gadget if you don't want to. Mark how far you have gone and how long it took you to go there. Since you will run two miles without walking by the end of the week, monitor how your pace affects your body. Though you may be training for a race, the training in and of itself is not timed. Do what feels right with your body and take advantage of the free running day to explore how far you can go.

Week 2	
"My grandmother started walking five miles a day when she was sixty. She's ninety-seven now, and we don't know where the heck she is." *-Ellen Degeneres*	
Day 8 (2 miles)	Run ¾ mile Walk ¼ mile *Repeat once*
Day 9	Rest
Day 10 (2 miles)	Run ¾ mile Walk ¼ mile *Repeat once*
Day 11	Free running
Day 12 (2 miles)	Run 2 miles *No walking*
Day 13	Rest
Day 14 (2 miles)	Run 2 miles *No walking*

Week three is the halfway point of the training. You have already experienced an incredible rise in pace, but you can handle it if you pay attention to the warning signs in your body. Take time after each run to gently massage your muscles or take a hot bath to help your muscles relax. Develop a dependence on drinking water while you run. Running long distances is hard on the body, and the water you lose in sweat needs replenishing with water. Always carry a water bottle with you to help fight dehydration.

Week 3	
"An early-morning walk is a blessing for the whole day." -Henry David Thoreau	
Day 15 (3 miles)	Run 1 ¼ miles Walk ¼ mile Repeat once
Day 16	Rest
Day 17 (3 miles)	Run 1 ¼ miles Walk ¼ miles Repeat once
Day 18	Free running
Day 19 (3 miles)	Run 3 miles No walking
Day 20	Rest
Day 21 (3 miles)	Run 3 miles No walking

Week four is designed to push you to your limit. You have already done a majority of the work: you are more than halfway through. That means that you can push yourself to the end of the course.

Rub ice on shin splints if they start to develop after long high-impact running. Reduce inflammation through compression and icing any aches when they occur. Take note of your posture and make sure that you are running correctly both be efficient and prevent injuries.

Week 4	
"If you are in a bad mood go for a walk. If you are still in a bad mood go for another walk." *-Hippocrates*	
Day 22 (4 miles)	Run 1 ½ miles Walk ½ mile *Repeat once*
Day 23	Rest
Day 24 (4 miles)	Run 1 ½ miles Walk ½ mile *Repeat once*
Day 25	Free running
Day 26 (4 miles)	Run 4 miles *No walking*
Day 27	Rest
Day 28 (4 miles)	Run 4 miles *No walking*

You have reached the final week. Congratulations! All that is left is to run until you reach your goal. Monitor how long it takes you to complete the first half of the week, and then continue to monitor your progress after you conclude.

Week 5	
"The trouble with jogging is that, by the time you realize you're not in shape for it, it's too far to walk back." *-Franklin P. Jones*	
Day 29 (5 miles)	Run 2 ¼ miles Walk ¼ mile *Repeat once*
Day 30	Rest
Day 31 (5 miles)	Run 2 ¼ miles Walk ¼ mile *Repeat once*
Day 32	Free running
Day 33 (5 miles)	Run 5 miles *No walking*
Day 34	Rest
Day 35 (5 miles)	Run 5 miles *No walking*

Conclusion

In today's world, running is not nearly as important as it has been in the past. We do not need to run for food, shelter, or often to protect our lives. Running has become a sport that tests the rate of human survival. Many people train for years to compete in some of the world's most celebrated racing competitions from marathons to the Olympics. High schools, universities, and even backyard games use running as part of the human experience.

Running has been part of the human race since the dawn of time, and it continues to be one of the most influential sports in the world because it challenges human endurance. The speed humans can achieve, and the distance they can reach has been compared throughout history. It is through these competitions that people have found the joys of running, and so can you.

Running is one of the most important sports for humans because it is in our blood, and it is vastly important to rediscover the effects running can have on the body. The world is becoming less interested in exercise because it is difficult and often unnecessary in everyday life. However, this is why we need running the most. It connects the body to the mind and creates a healthy lifestyle for all runners.

Running is highly beneficial to both the brain and the body. Running creates endorphins in the brain, causing feelings of happiness throughout the body. That is why many runners experience a "runner's high" when they take off. These endorphins reset hormonal imbalances in the brain, often temporarily curing feelings of anxiety and depression. Running also helps the brain learn faster, as brain cells make connections during physical exercise. In doing so, the brain is better able to remember, creating a defense against an aging brain. Running and exercise also prevent brain shrinkage, which affects how well the brain performs at older ages.

Running has also been known to help unhealthy cravings and addictions. Studies have shown that the brain does not experience such intense craving even after 30 minutes of exercise per week, making it a helpful aid to the cure for addiction. Runners see the benefits of better sleep that comes from heavy training, often improving any self-esteem issues and producing healthy bodies.

To create a healthy body, remember the correct way to feed it. It is not enough to eat just any type of food to gain energy; your diet influences how much energy you receive and how well you perform when out on the track. Protein, carbohydrates, and healthy fats are all essential to creating a healthy diet that will ensure gained endurance on runs. The Running Commandments should influence you to space out your meals and ensure you receive all of your nutrients you can get from them. However, no diet is perfect, and many use supplements to offset the inconsistencies in a poor diet. If you are not receiving enough supplements, you will not see the best results when running, and it is often more difficult to recover from long training sessions.

If you remember nothing else in this book, remember that water is one of your greatest allies, and to drink it often. Do not sacrifice water in favor of sports drinks or caffeinated beverages. Drink water while running and before and after a workout to give the body what it needs to continue to function properly.

When looking for the right equipment, there is so much more to consider than simply what looks good on the body. Shoes are the runner's most important equipment, and if you do not select shoes that complement your feet as you run, it could lead to injury. Know the value of your running shoe by making price comparisons and finding reviews in which to base your information. Even though cheaper shoes may seem like a good choice in a pinch, they often lead to injury, making them not worth the risk. Study how your feet hit the pavement when determining which shoe to buy to get the most out of every stride. Remember that the way your foot strikes the ground may require you to find shoes specialized to your feet. Do not be afraid to wait on a pair of running shoes if it means that they are the perfect pair for you.

The clothes you wear are also important when you head outside. To prevent sweat from sticking to your body, invest in clothing with moisture-wicking and quick-dry features. The clothing you wear should be able to protect you from the elements. So, if you are running a race outside and will be exposed to the sun for hours, choose a material that protects you from the sun. Find clothing that has inner liners to make running more comfortable and to warm you in the winter. The socks you wear help to prevent blisters and improve the cushioning of your feet against the pavement, so be aware that you are purchasing the right pair. Skip the sweatpants, heavy layers, and worn-out shoes in favor of running in attire that will both cover your body and prevent injury.

Warm-ups are essential to starting a run out the right way. You need to know your body and give it the time it needs to warm-up correctly. Though there is no prescribed time to warm-up, it is wise to spend at least ten minutes every time you head out the door. The first mile should also be a warm-up for your body. As soon as you pass that point, you can continue a rigorous regimen. Without it, you may be subjecting your body to injury.

Correct technique while running will not only make it more comfortable, but you will also see a change in the efficiency of your exercise. Positioning your head and neck appropriately keeps your body from displaying signs of wear. Since air pressure pulls your head down, forcing your head downward makes the rest of your body compensate to help you run effectively. Swinging your arms and your hands also propel you forward as you run. It is essential to build a strong core while running. The muscles in your core control the rest of your body so it is essential to keep those muscles healthy. The lower portion of your body propels our body forward, so maintain a straight posture while running to avoid injury.

While warm-ups are about getting your body warm for running using dynamic exercises, cool downs focus on two parts: aerobic and stretching cool downs. Each is required to get the most out of your workout and prevent injury. Keep your body primed for your next run, and make sure that you are careful about how you stretch. Do not bounce when stretching, and use your time to boost your performance for your next run.

Fatigue can help propel you forward if you use it correctly. When muscles tear, they do not allow your body to produce the same amount of force when intact. Therefore, as you continue your exercises, you push your body more as you run, making your body burst with more power the next time you run. However, be careful about how much you exercise. If you tear muscles too much, they become useless, and it takes days, if not weeks, to get back to where you were before. Eat and drink well to continue to fuel your body while you push forward.

Finally, be aware of what injures your body. The five central injuries common to runners are runner's knee, hamstring pulls, shin splints, piriformis syndrome, and Achilles tendonitis. As long as you take care of your body before and after every run and maintain a constant level of proper posture, you should not suffer from these injuries. It is up to you, then, to prevent your body from becoming injured.

How you run is up to you, but the answer is clear: running helps you both body and mind. If you follow the running plans in Chapter 9, you will be able to meet your running goals and challenge yourself to others along the way. The programs are for beginners, so as you improve, you may think they are too easy for you. However, they are a great place to start.

With this book, you will be able to run as much as you like and avoid the injury and nutritional pitfalls that beset many beginners. You will be able to run without fear of failure if you follow all of the steps listed. *Running for Beginners: The Training Guide to Run Properly, Get in Shape and Enjoy Your Body* will keep you on track when you struggle, and propel you forward with everything you need to know. If you keep this guide with you, you will always have the information you need for running now and in the future. The principles and tips listed are not just for those who are just beginning, but for everyone.

This book was written to help you succeed. Running can be difficult if you have not always enjoyed exercising, but this book will help you make it fun and keep you coming back for more. Any question you have about running has an answer here. With all this knowledge behind your back, head out to the track and make the most of your running career. And as they say, Godspeed my friends!

References

Abbate, E. (2019, May 23). The 5 most common running injuries and how to fix them. Retrieved February 12, 2020, from https://www.gq.com/story/5-most-common-running-injuries

Abundance & Health. (2018, April 12). Can Acetyl L-Carnitine really push you to the finish line? Retrieved February 8, 2020, from https://www.abundanceandhealth.co.uk/en/blog/post/112-can-acetyl-l-carnitine-really-push-you-to-the-finish-line

Allen, D. G., Lamb, G. D., & Westerblad, H. (2008). Skeletal muscle fatigue: Cellular mechanisms. Physiological Reviews, 88(1), 287–332. https://doi.org/10.1152/physrev.00015.2007

Arnarson, A., PhD. (2017, June 12). 10 evidence-based health benefits of whey protein. Retrieved February 8, 2020, from https://www.healthline.com/nutrition/10-health-benefits-of-whey-protein#section10

Asics. (2017, September 9). 6 ways to combat leg fatigue from running. Retrieved February 12, 2020, from https://www.asics.com/us/en-us/blog/article/combat-fatigue-and-tired-legs-from-running

Baker, L. (2003, April 12). Female runners eating a low-fat diet may increase risk of injury, limit energy supplies, UB study suggests. Retrieved February 7, 2020, from http://www.buffalo.edu/news/releases/2003/04/6181.html

Boerner, C. (2011, March 4). Exercise can curb marijuana use and cravings. Retrieved February 3, 2020, from https://news.vanderbilt.edu/2011/03/04/exercise-can-curb-marijuana-use-and-cravings/

Braun, P. (2016, January 4). Do you have a zinc deficiency? Why athletes should pay attention to zinc. Retrieved February 9, 2020, from https://blog.insidetracker.com/do-you-have-a-zinc-deficiency-why-athletes-should-pay

Breus, M. J. (2013, September 6). Better sleep found by exercising on a regular basis. Retrieved February 6, 2020, from https://www.psychologytoday.com/us/blog/sleep-newzzz/201309/better-sleep-found-exercising-regular-basis-0

Brooks, A. (2019, March 27). Krill oil: Happy runner knees. Retrieved February 8, 2020, from https://www.runtothefinish.com/krill-oil-happy-runner-knees/

Bruning, B. K. (2017, November 27). What runners should know about protein. Retrieved February 7, 2020, from https://www.active.com/nutrition/articles/what-runners-should-know-about-protein

Buttaccio, J. (2018, March 5). 4 benefits of magnesium and why runners should consider taking it. Retrieved February 9, 2020, from https://runsmartonline.com/blog/4-benefits-magnesium-why-runners-consider-supplementing/

Byrnes, H. (2016, April 23). How running can help with anxiety disorders. Retrieved January 30, 2020, from https://www.theactivetimes.com/run-race/n/how-running-can-help-anxiety-disorders

Cambro, E. (2019, March 22). The truth about runner's high: Everything you need to know. Retrieved January 28, 2020, from https://rockay.com/blog/runners-high/

Dack, D. (2019, February 15). How to cool down properly after a run. Retrieved February 11, 2020, from https://www.runnersblueprint.com/how-to-cool-down-properly-after-a-run/

Daniloff, C. (2017, June 9). Why running could be the answer to beating addiction. Retrieved February 3, 2020, from https://www.runnersworld.com/uk/health/mental-health/a775765/why-running-could-be-the-answer-to-beating-addiction/

Davis, J. (2018, February 26). Will supplementing with calcium help you avoid stress fractures. Retrieved February 8, 2020, from https://runnersconnect.net/calcium-and-stress-fractures/

Feller, A. K., & Fetters, K. A. (2019, March 26). 12 benefits of running that make you healthier (and happier). Retrieved February 5, 2020, from https://www.shape.com/fitness/cardio/11-science-backed-reasons-running-really-good-you?

Fernandez, E. (2010, May 26). Brief exercise reduces impact of stress on cell aging, UCSF study shows. Retrieved January 30, 2020, from https://www.ucsf.edu/news/2010/05/98475/brief-exercise-reduces-impact-stress-cell-aging-ucsf-study-shows

Fieseler, C. (2018, September 1). Are you suffering from an iron deficiency? Retrieved February 9, 2020, from https://www.runnersworld.com/uk/nutrition/supplements/a775183/why-iron-is-essential-for-runners/

Fitzgerald, S. (2016, January 18). Should you take a multivitamin? Retrieved February 8, 2020, from https://www.podiumrunner.com/nutrition/should-you-take-a-multivitamin/

Gaudette, B. J. (2013, October 4). How runners can benefit from fatigue. Retrieved February 12, 2020, from https://www.active.com/running/articles/how-runners-can-benefit-from-fatigue?page=2

Goodman, D. (2015, July 6). Health benefits of krill oil: 5 ways the supplement trumps regular fish oil. Retrieved February 8, 2020, from https://www.foxnews.com/health/health-benefits-of-krill-oil-5-ways-the-supplement-trumps-regular-fish-oil

Hadfield, J. (2016, August 5). 4 reasons for training fatigue. Retrieved February 12, 2020, from https://www.runnersworld.com/uk/training/a775127/4-reasons-for-training-fatigue/

Herbst, S. (2014, May 7). Why you need a strong core for running. Retrieved February 10, 2020, from https://blog.runkeeper.com/1657/why-you-need-a-strong-core-for-running/

Hogan, C. L., Mata, J., & Carstensen, L. L. (2013). Exercise holds immediate benefits for affect and cognition in younger and older adults. Psychology and Aging, 28(2), 587–594. https://doi.org/10.1037/a0032634

Kapoor, A. (2017, January 23). 8 glutamine rich foods and how they can boost your muscle strength. Retrieved February 8, 2020, from https://food.ndtv.com/food-drinks/8-glutamine-rich-foods-and-how-they-can-boost-your-muscle-strength-1651641

Kelly, J. (2020, January 27). How leg workouts for runners work. Retrieved February 10, 2020, from https://adventure.howstuffworks.com/outdoor-activities/running/training/leg-workouts-for-runners1.htm

Labelle, P. C. (2015, October 13). How to relax your shoulders while running. Retrieved February 10, 2020, from http://biomechanicssrc.com/how-to-relax-your-shoulders-while-running/

Lindsay, M. (2018, April 24). How arm swing affects your running efficiency. Retrieved February 10, 2020, from https://blog.mapmyrun.com/how-arm-swing-affects-your-running-efficiency/

Lobby, B. M. (2018a, January 25). Why you need to warm-up before running. Retrieved February 9, 2020, from https://www.active.com/running/articles/why-you-need-to-warm-up-before-running

Lobby, B. M. (2018b, September 5). How to Treat and Prevent Runner's Knee. Retrieved February 12, 2020, from https://www.active.com/running/articles/how-to-treat-and-prevent-runner-s-knee?page=2

Loria, K. (2016, November 4). Exercise might be more than good for your brain — it could make you more creative as well. Retrieved March 2, 2020, from https://www.businessinsider.com/exercise-benefits-brain-creativity-stress-2016-11

Luff, C. (2019, August 18). The best running clothes & gear for beginners. Retrieved February 9, 2020, from https://www.verywellfit.com/basic-running-clothes-for-beginners-2911840

Matzinger, G. (2017, October 6). Training tips: How cooling down can help you run faster times. Retrieved February 11, 2020, from https://www.runtastic.com/blog/en/cool-down-after-running/

Miller, J. A. (n.d.). How to feed a runner. Retrieved February 9, 2020, from https://www.nytimes.com/guides/well/healthy-eating-for-runners

Mitchell, M. (2018, January 1). Most read article of 2017: Heels or toes: What is the best way to run? Retrieved February 11, 2020, from https://fl.milesplit.com/articles/112223/most-read-article-of-2017-heels-or-toes-what-is-the-best-way-to-run

Mosman, M. (n.d.). Recovery benefits of L-Carnitine for endurance athletes. Retrieved February 8, 2020, from https://endurelite.com/blogs/free-nutrition-supplement-and-training-articles-for-runners-and-cyclists/recovery-benefits-of-l-carnitine-for-endurance-athletes

Mueller, S. (2020, January 18). 60 inspiring and motivating running quotes. Retrieved February 11, 2020, from http://www.planetofsuccess.com/blog/2017/motivating-running-quotes/

Natmessnig, R. (2018, June 14). How warming up improves your running performance. Retrieved February 10, 2020, from https://www.runtastic.com/blog/en/how-warming-up-improves-your-race-performance/

Norris, O. O. R. L. @. (2016, August 3). Why you should be eating healthy fats as a runner. Retrieved February 7, 2020, from https://lauranorrisrunning.com/benefits-of-healthy-fats-for-runners/

Performance Health. (n.d.). Runners: How to treat & prevent hamstring pain. Retrieved February 12, 2020, from https://www.performancehealth.com/articles/runners-how-to-treat-prevent-hamstring-pain

Preidt, R. (2019, November 5). Running -- even a little -- helps you live longer. Retrieved February 6, 2020, from https://www.webmd.com/fitness-exercise/news/20191105/run-for-your-life-new-study-recommends

Presland, C. (2017, December 31). 3 ways that running boosts your creativity. Retrieved February 3, 2020, from https://authorunlimited.com/blog/running-and-creativity

Ramdene, H. B. (2017, March 19). The beginner's guide to meal planning: What to know, how to succeed, and what to skip. Retrieved February 8, 2020, from https://www.thekitchn.com/the-beginners-guide-to-meal-planning-what-to-know-how-to-succeed-and-what-to-skip-242413

REI. (n.d.). What to wear running. Retrieved February 9, 2020, from https://www.rei.com/learn/expert-advice/running-clothing.html

Road Runner Sports. (n.d.). Couch potato to marathon champ: Your guide to the perfect running form. Retrieved February 11, 2020, from https://www.roadrunnersports.com/

Roche, D. (2018, June 11). The importance of starting slow. Retrieved February 10, 2020, from https://trailrunnermag.com/training/the-importance-of-starting-slow.html

Runner's World. (2014, July 14). 8 commandments of good running nutrition. Retrieved February 9, 2020, from https://www.runnersworld.com/uk/nutrition/a772005/8-commandments-of-good-running-nutrition/

Running Warehouse. (n.d.). How to pick running shoes. Retrieved February 9, 2020, from https://www.runningwarehouse.com/learningcenter/gear_gu ides/footwear/how_to_pick_running_shoes.html

Schmalz, D. L., Deane, G. D., Birch, L. L., & Davison, K. K. (2007). A longitudinal assessment of the links between physical activity and self-esteem in early adolescent non-Hispanic females. Journal of Adolescent Health, 41(6), 559–565. https://doi.org/10.1016/j.jadohealth.2007.07.001

Shmerling, R. H. (2018, April 13). Ask Dr. Rob about piriformis syndrome. Retrieved February 13, 2020, from https://www.health.harvard.edu/diseases-and-conditions/ask-dr-rob-about-piriformis-syndrome

Sifferlin, A. (2012, October 23). Exercise trumps brain games in keeping our minds intact. Retrieved January 30, 2020, from https://healthland.time.com/2012/10/23/exercise-trumps-brain-games-in-keeping-our-minds-intact/?utm_source=huffingtonpost.com&utm_medium=referral&utm_campaign=pubexchange_article

Sinrich, J. (2019, June 28). How running builds bone strength. Retrieved February 5, 2020, from https://aaptiv.com/magazine/running-build-bone-strength

Sooter, A. (2019, March 29). Running for depression: A natural & effective therapy. Retrieved January 28, 2020, from https://rockay.com/blog/running-for-depression/

Spade, M. (2018, May 14). Why you should be taking: L-Glutamine. Retrieved February 8, 2020, from https://tryabouttime.com/blogs/news-fitness/why-you-should-be-taking-glutamine

Stipp, D. (2012, June 4). All men can't jump. Retrieved February 5, 2020, from https://slate.com/culture/2012/06/long-distance-running-and-evolution-why-humans-can-outrun-horses-but-cant-jump-higher-than-cats.html

TGR Trail Running. (2017, June 26). Benefits of BCAA supplements for runners. Retrieved February 8, 2020, from https://tgr.run/2017/06/26/benefits-of-bcaa-supplements-for-runners/

The Huffington Post UK. (2014, January 31). A brilliant reason to start running: It can help reduce junk food cravings, nutritionists say. Retrieved February 5, 2020, from https://www.huffingtonpost.co.uk/2014/01/31/running-can-help-junk-food-cravings

Thelliez, V. (2019, October 31). Is Glutamine Essential for Runners? Retrieved February 8, 2020, from https://running-care.com/en/blog/2019/10/31/is-glutamine-essential-for-runners/

Thoreson, S. (2017, March 17). Nutrition: Why it matters when training. Retrieved February 7, 2020, from https://healthcare.utah.edu/healthfeed/postings/2017/03/marathon-nutrition.php

Vogt, V. (2020, January 27). How core strength training for runners works. Retrieved February 10, 2020, from https://adventure.howstuffworks.com/outdoor-activities/running/training/core-strength-training-runners2.htm

Why and how to cool down. (2017, September 17). Retrieved February 11, 2020, from https://runnersconnect.net/running-questions/why-and-how-to-cool-down/

Why fatigue is a necessary part of training and how to manage it. (2019, August 23). Retrieved February 12, 2020, from https://runnersconnect.net/coach-corner/how-to-manage-fatigue-and-why-it-is-necessary/

Why weak glutes are a runner's biggest enemy and how you can fix. (2019, December 19). Retrieved February 10, 2020, from https://middleagemarathoner.com/weak-glutes/

Williams, P. T. (2013). Effects of running and walking on osteoarthritis and hip replacement risk. Medicine & Science in Sports & Exercise, 45(7), 1292–1297. https://doi.org/10.1249/mss.0b013e3182885f26

Winter, B., Breitenstein, C., Mooren, F. C., Voelker, K., Fobker, M., Lechtermann, A., Knecht, S. (2007). High impact running improves learning. Neurobiology of Learning and Memory, 87(4), 597–609. https://doi.org/10.1016/j.nlm.2006.11.003

Printed in Great Britain
by Amazon

42214436R00108